LAURA SHILLITOE DICAPRIO

Letters to Freddie

The Biography of Midge Thomas

Letters to Freddie

The Biography of Midge Thomas

Acknowledgments

This book was made possible by:

- Generous grants from:

  - Panther Graphics, Inc.

  - Panther Solutions, LLC

  - Flower City Group, Inc.

- Encouragement from my uncle, George Scharr

- Inspiration from Midge Thomas

Thank you!

Midge Thomas and George Scharr enjoy dinner together at a restaurant on University Avenue in Rochester, NY, summer 2022.

Contents

ノ〜

February 10, 2023

Dear Laura,

I must thank God first for bringing you into this elderly time space in my life. God answered my prayers to tell someone about my meaning of a calling and made an interesting and beautiful spiritual connection through George Scharr (one of my 1987 Freddie Thomas Foundation dedicated volunteers) about an opportunity for you to interview me to write an article in *(585) Magazine*. Soon after the publication, this story immediately motivated you to publish your first book not only telling my historical involvement in the City of Rochester but also on an international recognition of what my late husband, Dr. Freddie Thomas, and I meant to our community. About fifty years of my volunteer services was after his death in February 1974.

Laura, your time and energy has not been in vain. We award you with a big THANK YOU as the author and publisher of this book. It was an important period of time, people, and events in Rochester's history. I would like this book to be listed as a living memorial of contributions from my late parents, Milton and Ethel Banks, my two brothers, Charles and George Banks, my sister, Helen Corley, and my late husband, Dr. Freddie Thomas. It also is an opportunity for each reader to capture some of the memories of my family.

I was surprised to receive a letter on July 19th from Marquis Publications' *Who's Who in America* stating that your article titled "A Creative Visionary" captured their attention in *(585) Magazine* and that on June 23, 2022, my candidacy was approved and I am being considered as a biographical candidate in the next upcoming edition of *Who's Who in America*. Congratulations to you, Laura.

I'm getting several comments from that article published in the January/February 2022 issue. It's so easy that friends can immediately find your story on their cell phones when they Google the article. I give my sincere *thanks and appreciation* to each of my volunteers and financial contributors.

Sincerely,

MT

Preface

I first met Midge Thomas in October 2021 while on a freelance assignment for a local Rochester, New York, magazine. My uncle, George Scharr, had suggested that I write an article about his friend Midge, a woman who dedicated her life to improving her community in memory of her late husband, Dr. Freddie Thomas. I performed some light research before our interview and gathered a general sense of her accomplishments through various local news stories and newspaper articles I found archived online. From what I read, Midge was best known for starting the Freddie Thomas Foundation in honor of her late husband, a not-for-profit organization that has contributed to numerous community betterment projects since its inception in 1974.

The moment I arrived at Midge's apartment for our scheduled interview, it was apparent that my preliminary research had only provided background on a fraction of Midge's societal contributions.

Over fifty framed awards, certificates, and recognitions lined the walls and shelves of her entryway, and sandwiched in between them were photographs of Midge standing beside former mayors, local congressmen and -women, and a variety of organizational board members. In addition, three, five-inch binders sat on her dining room table, each one stuffed with news articles and photos chronicling the hundreds of projects she tackled in her 95 years. And in preparation for our interview, she had compiled an Excel spreadsheet full of names and contact information of people she had worked with over the years. Clearly, this was a woman with a robust history and stories to tell.

I went home after our interview, wrote the 1,200-word article, and submitted it to my editor, but I didn't feel the same sense of completion I usually get after finishing a piece. So many stories she shared with me during our two hours together didn't make it into the article. I felt like these stories needed to be told and that all of her accomplishments needed to be recognized. Her list of achievements included starting and owning two businesses before turning 40, establishing the Dr. Freddie Thomas Foundation, turning an abandoned, 120,000-square-foot building into a thriving public community center, donating a water fountain to downtown Rochester so that everyone had access to fresh, clean water, and mentoring hundreds of students during her lifetime, many of whom still refer to her as their adoptive mother.

All of Midge's projects had the underlying theme of bettering the Rochester, New York community, and she won many awards and recognitions through the years. She was awarded a National Jefferson Award (1982), was inducted into the National Women's Hall of Fame (2003), and had multiple Rochester mayors declare "Midge Thomas" days in recognition of her accomplishments. Midge is quite literally a nationally recognized patriot of Rochester.

After the magazine article was published in November 2021, I carefully clipped it out and included it in my portfolio. I had written dozens of articles in my 10 years as a freelance writer, but this was the first published piece that felt unfinished. Midge had enough stories and accomplishments to fill a book, and I wanted to be the one to tell her story.

With George's encouragement, we visited Midge on a Saturday morning in January 2022 for breakfast and to discuss the idea of me penning her biography. She was thrilled to be asked and gratefully accepted. She had assisted in the research process in the biography of her late husband a few years prior, so she was familiar with the lengthy process and dedication needed to produce a book.

Along with being a philanthropist, Midge is a captivating story-teller and information hoarder, which really helped me during the research phase of this project. During the first few months, I visited her every week with a topic and a list of questions, and she would spend hours telling me stories from her past. Many sessions ended with an informational hand-off, either a binder filled with newspaper articles and letters for my research or inspirational books for me to gain encouragement from as I became overwhelmed with the task.

As I was going through one of her binders one afternoon, I came across a small packet filled with letters she had written over the years to her late husband. The letters were heartfelt and candid, and Midge told me later that most were written late at night when she was alone and wanted to rekindle her connection with him. The letters touched on the different projects she worked on, and she reminded Freddie in each one that he was her inspiration behind each new initiative. I knew Freddie was the driving force behind many of Midge's impassioned projects, but it was reading these letters that sparked the flow for this book.

Each chapter of this biography opens with one of Midge's letters to Freddie, which provides insight into her mindset during that period of time in her life. The title of this book, *Letters to Freddie,* pays homage to those letters and Midge's promise to better the Rochester, New York, community through his name.

It has been an absolute joy working with Midge over the past year. I can finally say that I have the sense of completion I have been yearning for, knowing that Midge's story is finally told.

Chapter 1

Becoming Midge Banks Thomas

ᕲ

September 3, 1995

Dear Freddie,

Remember about 45 years ago, in May 1956, when we met at a mutual friend's birthday party? Within a year we dated, courted, became engaged, then shared 17 beautiful years of marriage.

Those years we dined together, exercised together, worked together, prayed together, made love, shared secrets, and shared our future dreams together until that one rainy morning when Dr. Perry Eck announced to both of us you were diagnosed with multiple myeloma. You were brave enough to question how long you had to live. I admired how you taught students while they cared for you on your sick bed. Upgrading their report cards from C's and D's to A's and A+, shocking their teachers.

Freddie, remember when we traveled, we took seniors, children, and friends on trips to Cleveland, Detroit, and Chicago? Some to New York City, Philly, Washington, Norfolk, and onto Greensboro, NC? It didn't cost much more and they were pleasant traveling friends.

I still remember how you treated Dad and Mother like kings and queens, and me, my monthly wedding anniversary gifts were so creative. I didn't see much of our dining room lace tablecloth because you used our dining room table for your research space, but I enjoyed entertaining those diplomats from the United Nations, senators and congressmen, as well as teaching youngsters how to eat properly at our table.

Freddie, many of those students have improved their lifestyles off of social services and drugs and are helping others. Your philosophy of setting an extra plate at our daily candlelit table was an excellent idea. When friends visited us they were welcome to share our meals with us.

Remember you taught friends to shop for used furniture to save their funds for higher goals such as becoming an early homeowner? Your homemade blackboard in our living room for teaching was like our priceless piece of furniture.

Yes, Freddie, you were a scholar, scientist, musician, lecturer, humanitarian, and, above all, an educator. I remember your quote, "Preparation in education is far more important than preparation in sports." You didn't just teach them, you inspired them to learn. I liked that approach to teaching.

Sincerely,

Midge

Becoming Midge Banks Thomas

Margaret Caroline Banks was born at Rochester General Hospital on September 1, 1926. She was the second child born to her parents, Milton and Ethel Banks. Her brother Charles was three years older, and younger siblings, Helen and George, would follow a few years later. The family lived in Mumford, New York, about twenty miles southwest of the city.

Milton Banks worked for the Ebsary Gypsum Block Company in Wheatland, about three miles from their home. He never missed a day of work in his twenty-three-year career. Ethel was a stay-at-home mother to her four children.

As a child, Margaret—or Midge, as her family called her—was fortunate to have built-in playmates with her siblings. All relatively close in age, there was always someone to adventure around the neighborhood on roller skates and bicycles, build mud pies decorated with wild berries in the backyard, or play inside with dolls and board games on rainy afternoons.

Ethel was adamant on instilling a strong work ethic in her children, which was not a hard task given that her children watched her work hard throughout the day. She assigned age-appropriate chores with high expectations, so in return the kids would feel like their roles were integral to the running of the household. Midge learned to cook from three family matriarchs—her mother, her Grandmother Banks, and her Grandmother Alston—and each morning she was expected to prepare coffee, a sandwich, and a dessert for her father's lunch pail. Throughout the week, Midge assisted her mother with making beds, sorting laundry, and setting the dinner table, and on Saturdays she cleaned the family's white shoes with shoe polish. One of her favorite chores was brushing the delicate fringe on the family's ornate oriental carpeting with a special brush.

Music was constantly playing in the Banks house, either on the radio or via a practice session echoing from one of the children's piano or vocal lessons. Midge's parents exposed the children to many musical genres at local concert venues and took them into the city to see bigger names like Cab Calloway, Duke Ellington, and Nat King Cole. Midge and her brothers were also fine dancers and would entertain the neighbors with their two-step.

Education was of utmost importance to Ethel and Milton. Bible meditations and lessons were held each night between seven p.m. and eight p.m. to ensure proper time was dedicated to studying. A family party was thrown for good report cards, and many parties were enjoyed throughout the years.

The Banks family loved company. They always had room at their holiday dinner table, and they welcomed guests with freshly polished silver, sparkling crystal goblets, and special china. The Banks family always prepared enough food to accommodate friends who dropped in, and welcomed their guests with roasts, home-canned fruits, and vegetables from Ethel's garden.

Midge graduated from Caledonia-Mumford High School in 1944 and went on to study cosmetology at the Rochester Adrianne School of Beauty Culture. Her father taught her how to drive in a 1946 Studebaker to ensure his daughter would continue to be independent and able to attend her classes.

Upon graduation from the Adrianne school, Midge took business classes at Rochester Business Institute and furthered her education with tailoring and sewing courses at the Rochester Institute of Technology and the Academy of Millinery Design in Orange, New Jersey.

A handful of men courted Midge over the years, but none of them struck Midge to be suitable enough to be her husband. She was not concerned with her single status, even as her friends became engaged and married off, because building her business was her main focus. After graduating with her cosmetology degree, Midge did not want to throw money away by renting a chair at someone else's salon. Instead, her father, who had always encouraged entrepreneurship in all four of his children, built her a one-room salon off the family's home. Her business, the Orchid Beauty Salon, was well-known throughout Mumford, New York, and neighboring districts, and she provided services to a steady flow of clients.

It was during this busy season of life, in May 1956, when 28-year-old Midge was invited to a friend's birthday party. Exhausted from a long week, and thinking of settling for a night in, instead, Midge reluctantly agreed to attend with a few of her girlfriends. She had no idea that her future husband was already at the party and that this night would forever change the trajectory of her life.

Across town at the party, Dr. Freddie Thomas was stationed by the snack and punch table, chatting with a friend. He'd been at the party for about an hour and was ready to go home. Freddie was a

38-year-old bachelor who had, up to this point, focused all his energy on his education and medical research career. A graduate of Albany Medical School, Class of 1952, he had recently accepted a full-time position with Eastman Kodak as a research technologist in the Emulsion and Research Division. He was the only Black scientist in the department, and the weight of this responsibility did not escape him. Throughout his time in medical school, he had faced discrimination and skepticism as a Black man in a White man's field, which only intensified his effort and determination. At the time, only about 15 percent of medical school graduates were African Americans, and Freddie was determined to positively impact that statistic.

As the conversation between Freddie and his companion died down, he was about to announce his departure when he noticed a young woman in a white dress enter the party. She was petite, with shoulder-length hair, but it was her confidence that struck him. Even from across the room, he could tell that something was different about her, and he was immediately drawn to her energy. He decided to stay at the party for a while longer to see if he could muster the courage to chat with her or even ask for a dance.

When the song *Treasure of Love*, by Clyde McPhatter, started to play, Freddie turned to his friend and said, "See that lady in the white dress? She's going to be my wife." Leaving his companion at the punch table, Freddie found the courage to finally approach Midge, and they started the first of many dances together that evening.

Perhaps it was foreshadowing, with Midge dressed in white and Freddie in his going-out suit, but the two seemed destined to get married from that first encounter. They were bonded from that evening forward and shared a brief, intense courtship that met with Ethel and Milton's approval. Four months later, on September 1, 1956, Midge's birthday, Freddie slipped a diamond ring on her finger and asked her to officially be his bride.

Nine months later, on the morning of her wedding, a time when most brides would be fussing with their hair or getting a fresh manicure, Midge and her mother were driving around Rochester looking for a locksmith who could make a key to fit her vintage luggage set for her upcoming honeymoon. It was the early morning of Saturday, February 9, 1957, and Midge's wedding was due to start in a few hours. Time worked against them as they combed the streets.

This last-minute lock-and-key mission was a result of Midge's impulsive fiancé, who surprised her the night before with tickets to Bermuda. Freddie had scrapped their original honeymoon plans to visit family along the frigid East Coast in favor of a more exotic vacation for his new bride. These last minute travel plans caused Midge to upend her packed suitcase full of turtlenecks and wool pants and frantically rummage through the bottom of her dressers in search of the summer clothes she had stored away months before at the season's end.

Midge and her mother finally found an open shop, and having secured a key for her luggage, the two raced to the church. The ceremony was to take place at the AME Zion Church, the same place Midge and Freddie had met just a few months earlier.

Midge's mother had found the perfect, second-hand lace wedding dress a few weeks prior while combing the classifieds, and as Midge dressed, she could hear the 500 guests arriving and milling about outside the bridal suite.

Although Midge was nervous for the ceremony to begin, and about being on display for so many people, she was steadfast in her decision to marry Freddie, for no beau had ever cherished her the way he did.

The Thomases celebrated every day they had together, but the ninth of each month was special. The ninth was their monthly anniversary, a day to remember their love, their wedding, and their commitment to one another. Every month, Freddie splurged on elaborate gifts for his wife: jewelry and perfume, and fabric from his travels to New York City, which Midge sewed into unique suits and dresses. The gifts were always accompanied by a handwritten letter or card, a way for Freddie to remind Midge of his love and devotion no matter how busy his work schedule became.

They shared many professional accomplishments during their years together. Freddie worked his way up from research technologist to research assistant, to a research associate at The University of Rochester School of Medicine and Dentistry. He gave lectures on cell biology throughout the United States, Canada, Bermuda, and France, and was an active member in many scientific research groups.

Midge expanded upon her salon experience and opened a second business, Original Creations Bridal Accessories, where she designed and made bridal hats, veils, and other fashion accessories. Noticing a lack of support for African American women-owned businesses in the area, she co-founded The Rochester Club of the National Association of Negro Business and Professional Women's Clubs, Inc., which later became the Rochester Genesee Valley of NANBPW Inc. She became its president in 1958 and often hosted meetings in her home. She was the group's third president and grew the club to eighty-one members.

The mission of The Rochester Genesee Valley Club was to provide development opportunities, resources, and collaboration opportunities to Black professional women. Workshops, speaking engagements, and mentorship programs were made available year round. "I always tell young ladies to get a career and not a job," Midge reported. "If you get a career, you can work for your passion and have a job, too."

As busy as they were with their careers, Midge and Freddie's passion project was bettering their Rochester community. They were a young, powerful, successful couple who were capable of making a difference in the lives of those less fortunate, and they embraced this sense of duty.

Unbeknownst to the Thomases, when they bought their first home, a two-story 1900s' Colonial in the heart of downtown Rochester, they were taking part in a tremendous growth era for the African American community in the city. Between 1950 and 1960, the Black population had increased 211 percent and now accounted for 7.4 percent of the city's total population. Rochester's economic growth was also expanding during this time, due largely in part to the rapid developments with Eastman Kodak Corporation and

Xerox. But the spike in growth in the two companies and in the Black population were independent of one another, for the majority of open positions at Kodak and Xerox required a college education.

Freddie and Midge recognized this disproportionate fact and decided to use their newly purchased home as a learning center for Rochester's young community. Their first home-renovation project focused on converting the den into a library. Freddie's collection of 5,000 books were displayed on floor-to-ceiling shelves that Midge had sourced from local thrift stores. Community members were encouraged to borrow from his collection.

In addition to the library, Freddie and Midge turned their living room into a makeshift classroom to further mentor and redirect Rochester's at-risk youth. Freddie would often strike up conversations with groups of students on his way home from work. He tried to pique their interest in subjects like history or science. Those struggling with their academics were invited into the Thomases' home for free tutoring, with Freddie taking notes on a homemade chalkboard made from a discarded refrigerator box. "The Thomas house on Skuse Street was a community center of knowledge with wall-to-wall and floor-to-ceiling shelves of books," noted reporter Adolph Dupree from *about...time* magazine. "A discarded carton was painted and used as a blackboard for high school dropouts and slow learners. The dining table was a conference center for distinguished scientists, clergy, historians, scholars, and people from every walk of life."

Midge supported Freddie's accumulation of bright, ambitious students, many of whom visited the Thomases daily. She assumed the role of a loving mother and mentor, a figure not present in many of their lives. She asked how their days were and followed along with their lessons, mentored them through their teenage angst, and supported their aspirations to better themselves through education. In the afternoons, Midge loaded up on half-priced cookies and brownies from the local bakery to provide as after-school snacks, a privilege that many of Freddie's students couldn't afford. Extras were stored in the freezer, available for a quick defrost if more food was needed.

In the evenings, after the students went home, the couple seldom dined alone. White or Black, politicians or non-voters, poor or financially stable, religious or atheist—everyone was welcome at the Thomas house, and an extra place was always set at the dinner table in case someone dropped in unannounced. Notable guests included US Senator Kenneth Keating (1959 – 1965) and Congresswoman Jessica "Judy" Weis (1959 – 1963).

The couple did not discriminate against who belonged to their social circle, the thought being that everyone added value to their lives. After dinner Midge and her friends would often sew or cook together while the men talked about their work or personal interests.

Midge always set a proper, matching table, complete with a lace tablecloth, folded cloth napkins, and candles, all inexpensive luxuries that looked elegant and made guests feel special. Any student who stayed for dinner was given an extra lesson in dinner manners, a life skill that Midge deemed necessary for a well-rounded individual.

In 1972, during the height of Freddie's lecturing career, he started suffering from sharp pains in his abdomen. When the discomfort could no longer be managed with over-the-counter painkillers, his general practitioner, Dr. Perry Eck with Rochester General Hospital, arranged a series of x-rays and bloodwork with a hematologist to diagnose his illness. In September 1972, at the age of 54, Freddie was diagnosed with multiple myeloma, a cancer of the plasma cells.

There are multiple contributing factors that increase the risk of multiple myeloma, including being an African American male and being exposed to radiation or certain chemicals in the workplace. Unfortunately, these boxes were all ticked for Freddie, whose years of hands-on research as a biochemist could have contributed as a catalyst. He was given two to three years to live.

Naturally, Midge was heartbroken. They had only shared 15 years together and felt as though their union had just begun. She had long quit her job managing both Orchid Salon and Original Creations Bridal Accessories to focus on their philanthropic projects and to be available to accompany Freddie on his lecturing tours, but seemingly overnight, that focus was shifted to being a caregiver.

Midge managed his medications, scheduled his chemotherapy sessions, and cared for him as he navigated the side effects of his treatments. Freddie was still able to lecture locally for a year after his diagnosis, until he became paralyzed and bedridden. He performed his last lecture, "The Black Race: Some Contributions to Civilizations," at the Rochester Museum and Science Center in 1973.

Midge set up a hospital bed in the living room classroom so that Freddie could continue to teach in his weakened state and be present for his cherished students. Current and former students set up a 24-hour-care rotation schedule with Midge so that someone could sit with the admired professor around the clock. Although in constant pain, Freddie looked forward to the steady stream of visitors and continued to teach on his good days.

Around the start of the new year in 1974, as Freddie's condition deteriorated, he and Midge had many intense but insightful private conversations about life and death. This was Freddie's way of preparing Midge for the inevitable and providing her with a sense of closure before he passed. Midge had never grieved during his illness but knew she had to prepare herself. She asked Freddie many times if she could record their final conversations together because his philosophies on life and death could benefit so many other people, but he always denied her request, saying, "Honey, these conversations are for you."

Midge gifted Freddie a dozen red roses on his 56th birthday on February 10, 1974, the last present she would buy for her husband. Freddie loved staring at the bouquet and requested that the vase be turned daily so he could take in the different views of the flowers.

Freddie was moved to Rochester General Hospital in February, and former students and colleagues were called in to say their last goodbyes. People flew in from as far away as Texas to pay their last respects, and Midge, although devastated, encouraged people not to cry in front of Freddie. When it became apparent that he was about to take his final breaths, Midge was left alone in the room to say her final goodbye. Freddie passed away on February 24, 1974, at the age of 56. Midge and Freddie had 17 wonderful years together.

Engagement photo of Midge Banks and Dr. Freddie Thomas, September 1956.

The decorated marriage certificate of Freddie Thomas and Midge Banks. Freddie's grandfather, James Thomas, purchased the ornate certificate for Freddie, his first grandson, when he was born on February 10, 1918. It was tucked away and presented to him on his wedding day on February 9, 1957, and both Midge and Freddie signed their promise to one another.

Thru The Looking Glass

At the Drop or a Hat!

By LOUISE WILSON

Louise Wilson is heard twelve times weekly on Station WHAM 9:10 and 9:25 A.M. Monday through Friday; 9:30 A.M. and 12:30 P.M. Saturday.

Though small in stature, she's giant-size when it comes to originality! That's Margaret Thomas who can design a new Easter bonnet "at the drop of a hat." She never designs two hats alike and thinks nothing of designing and creating as many as fifty hats for a single fashion show.

As the wife of a research assistant in plastic surgery, Margaret found time to study dressmaking from which came her interest in millinery. So she set about to take a course from the Academy of Millinery Designing and finished it much earlier than prescribed.

Mrs. Thomas' very first professional design was a three-way houndstooth wool hat some seven years ago. Since then she's gone on to create hat and shoe combinations, hat and scarf twosomes, hat and blouses, hats and pocketbooks, hat and dickeys, hats and gloves. But you notice—always—HATS.

Most recently, M a r g a r e t, whose label is MIDGE has branched out into the at-home fashions. This incredibly fertile and original mind seems to recognize no boundaries when it comes to creating in wonderfully, wearable originals.

dramatically manipulated brim, for instance.

Always a little ahead of her time, milliner Margaret did the square brim hat a good five years ago. Now, they're just coming into their own, she observes.

She's happy about the prophetic quality of her hats. They stay in style longer. When you realize she designs but one-of-a-kind hats — it's really quite amazing.

Some of Margaret Thomas' time is spent presenting hat party or hat shows, (program chairmen, take notice in planning next year's meetings) and she has exhibited in Rochester Buffalo, Princeton and Washington.

This may be an idea for many women's clubs who are looking for a new way to feature a fashion show. (He phone number is 546-4253).

With each of her original creations that Mrs. Thomas carefully packs into a stunning box, she includes a card certifying that the hat is an exclusive creation. "Just my guarantee they won't be seeing their hats on anyone else!"

Another special personalized service of this bright young woman is designing headpieces to match the gowns of the brides-to-be. Margaret Thomas will even go with the bride to see her gown in order to design a headpiece that will be complementary, whether of identical lace or fabric or both.

The finding of matching fabric takes a bit of time and sleuthing but somehow, she always succeeds.

So strongly does Mrs. Thomas believe in "the total look" that she often designs special hats for the mother of the bride and the mother of the groom.

One outstanding turban bearing the Midge label is convertible five ways. She uses brocades, lace, felt, feathers, fur, fabric, flowers, straws, leaves. One she created for me is a field of flowers and veiling in bright orange. It flatters the face without mussing the hair.

Her interest in promoting "the total look" extends to making a tweed hat and matching cape for chilly Spring days and evenings. For special occasions she has done a white sequinned cocktail hat. But almost none of her hats are to be worn one way—they convert magically.

Some of the Midge-labeled hats are of lush combinations such as brocade and mink. Others are pure line in straw, a tailored hat in straw with a

A Times-Union newspaper article featuring Midge's hat business, October 1968.

A portrait from a 1968 The Times-Union *newspaper article, featuring two of Midge's original hat designs*

A photo of Midge used in a 1969 newspaper article announcing her honorable mention for the Times-Union Club Woman of the Year award.

Midge sits with her sister, Helen, and her parents, Milton and Ethel Banks. The Banks family was awarded the Monroe County Family of the Year Award in 1984 and were honored at a luncheon at Rochester's Strathallan Hotel.

Chapter 2

The Freddie Thomas Foundation

September 14, 1976

Dearest Freddie,

I am in a dilemma and don't know who I can talk to or who should be talking to me. Tears are constantly flowing down my face most of this night. I just have the strength to take a tissue and continually wipe them away.

It is now 4:30 in the morning and I'm wondering if I made the right choice of living here in this building alone. And taking these responsibilities that must go along with it. I feel I need about two or three persons to be living in the center with me for protection, if necessary, or just for me to know that I'm not here alone.

I am afraid, especially after a few break-ins, ransacking, and stealing here and there. I am very much afraid.

I am also discouraged about the concern and things we believed and fought for. Remember our many hours spent fighting for the awareness and dignity for our people? Our marriage was so beautiful. Our sharing with each other was for people. I loved every minute of it all. I'm doing the same thing; however, I can't see how I can give any more. It's just about 5 –16 hours daily, giving energy in volunteering what limited capabilities I have here and everywhere possible.

Life is not the same without you. Being your widow is not getting easier, or I'm getting weaker. I know this is a temporary emotional feeling, but I miss you.

Your love,

Midge

The Freddie Thomas Foundation

Midge struggled to accept her newly assigned identity as a widow. Even during the first few months after Freddie's passing, with every aspect of his illness and death still fresh, she felt a sense of duty as the one left on this earth to continue his community-betterment agenda. At a time when she felt the societal expectations to stay at home to wallow in her grief, she knew that her healing would come from continuing to build out the educational and mentorship programs that she and Freddie had started together.

Many friends and previous students called and visited Midge during this time to see how she was coping. One friend, John Griffin, had remained particularly close to Freddie over the years and viewed him as a lifetime mentor. John became a successful real estate agent and attributed his success to Freddie, who had offered encouragement throughout his education and early career. John had many conversations with Freddie before his passing regarding his vision for bettering the Rochester community.

Before he passed away, Freddie confided in John that he regretted never investing in a proper facility to expand upon the intimate tutoring classroom he built in his home. The prospect of a larger space would have allowed Freddie to envision more staff volunteers and program offerings, but most importantly, a new facility would have meant that more young people would benefit from educational and mentoring assistance. He had envisioned a multi-purpose building that offered classrooms and recreational spaces, and he had begun to comb real estate listings looking for a perfect fit. One building that stood out to him was the former Jewish Community Center (JCC) located at 400 Andrews Street in downtown Rochester, but unfortunately, his illness rapidly progressed, and he became physically unable to pursue this lead.

When John recounted this conversation to Midge, she immediately knew that converting this building into a recreation center and haven for Rochester's community was her calling. It was more than an opportunity to fulfill her late husband's wishes, it was a chance to extend the reach of their mission and increase the number of lives they could positively impact.

Although it was in need of extensive renovations, Midge saw nothing but potential as she toured the seven-story, 120,000-square-foot facility. The brick building had been built in 1932 and offered 165 bedrooms with shared, dorm-style bathrooms, classrooms, an auditorium, gymnasiums, and a swimming pool.

"It was advertised as an architectural marvel," according to a *Rochester Patriot* magazine article from 1982. The article continued:

Several solid stories, plus a basement recreation area featuring a heated pool, sauna room, hand-ball courts, the works; an "acoustically perfect" auditorium that could seat a thousand; offices, a mall, 165 dorm rooms, a Cutler Chute and one of the last manually-operated elevators in town. To forward-thinking developers, the building probably seemed like a big red white elephant. But for Margaret Thomas, it was the perfect location for putting the philosophy of her late husband into action.

In order to fund the purchase of the building, and provide a mission and purpose behind its acquisition, Midge leaned into her late husband's desire to provide young people with a safe space to learn and grow. On July 9, 1974, the same year Freddie passed, the Freddie Thomas Foundation (FTF) was born.

The JCC, that had shown the building to a few other prospects, supported Midge's vision for the property and approved a swift sale of $198,000—down from its original asking price of $1.2 million. Midge filed for, and was awarded, a 501(c) (3) to assist with the purchase of the building. She renamed the building The Triangle Community Center.

Sanford J. Liebschutz, president of the JCC of Greater Rochester, chronicled his support in a letter to John, writing:

On behalf of the Board of Directors and the members of the Jewish Community Center of Greater Rochester, Inc., I wish to extend to the Freddie Thomas Foundation our best wishes for every future success on the occasion of the re-laying of the cornerstone and re-dedication of the Triangle Community Center. . . . When we learned of the interest of the Freddie Thomas Foundation in acquiring the building to operate a new community center, we were most happy that we could make arrangements for you to acquire it. It gives us great satisfaction to know that once again our former home is dedicated to serving the cultural and recreational needs of the residents of the urban center, helping them to deal with the realities and concerns of everyday life, as it did for members of the Jewish community for many years. The goals of the Freddie Thomas Foundation and the Triangle Community Center deserve the support of the entire Greater Rochester Community. You may be assured that you have ours.

Midge named the new building the Triangle Community Center (TCC) as both a commentary on the building's shape and the three pillars it would represent: recreation, education, and cultural activities. "My husband spoke in terms of our social fabric, a tapestry," Midge explained to *about…time* magazine in 1978. "I believe TCC could play a major role in aiding individuals to become productive, contributing citizens."

The official mission of the FTF was to help both individuals and non-profit organizations, and now Midge had a space large enough to cater to both. It was incorporated as a not-for-profit corporation, exempt from federal income tax as a charitable organization.

Midge realized that she would be unable to run the Foundation and building by herself, so she appointed John as the co-founder of the FTF and executive director of the TCC. Together, the two developed a philosophy for the facility, which was "to provide facilities for recreation, entertainment, and other wholesome activities and to provide a location for cultural activities, artistic exhibits, and community meeting facilities, particularly for inner-city and low- and moderate-income persons."

Like Midge, John knew the TCC had the potential to drastically improve Rochester's downtown social and educational scene, but the reality of the expenses required for the building's upkeep remained at the forefront of his mind. He worried, saying, "The downtown-area revitalization agencies can only help themselves by helping us. The community has an 'obligation and responsibility' to support our efforts here. Beyond financial concerns, because of our displayed commitment, we should receive moral support of the community."

They recruited two more full-time volunteers, both friends of theirs, to help run the facility: Bessie Stallworth was appointed volunteer director and Olivia Reid assumed a position as secretary. A team of administrative assistants included Phil Fedele, Eric Strader, Robert Tobin, and Ruby Smith. A 13-member board of directors was appointed to advise Midge and John, and additional volunteers were recruited from organizations that included The Work Experience Program, Catholic Youth Organization, Community Aid Program, and Volunteers in Service.

Community Development issued a grant of $77,300 for rehabilitation, such as the installation of fire walls. One volunteer, Terri Miller, raised $7,000 to refurbish the main lounge, which in turn was named the Terri Lounge. Midge moved into the janitor's apartment on the fourth floor of the complex to be available at all times to monitor the extensive renovation process. The living quarters covered about 800 square feet, divided into a living room, bedroom, bathroom, and a small kitchenette. Through renovations, decorating, and moving in her personal belongings, the apartment quickly began to feel like home.

The TCC was mostly empty those first few months of ownership, and oftentimes, Midge would be the only one within the entire building. Midge found it easy to preoccupy her mind during the day, but the loneliness she felt at night mirrored the emptiness of the building. But throughout the sleepless nights, the stress of starting up the FTF, and the cost of renovations, Midge never regretted her decision to purchase the TCC. As a creative visionary, she knew these stressors were a small price to pay, considering the positive impact the TCC and, ultimately, the FTF, would have on the Rochester community.

Midge Thomas and John Griffin, personal friend and president of the Freddie Thomas Foundation's board of directors, take inventory of Freddie Thomas's book collection.

The Triangle Community Center Building, located at 400 Andrews Street in Downtown Rochester, NY. The seven-story building was built in 1932 and offered 120,000 square feet of living and recreational space for the Freddie Thomas Foundation.

Chapter 3

The Triangle Community Center

October 11, 1976

Dearest Freddie:

Ever since you left two and a half years ago, I've been thinking about how we met and our experiences in life together. Remember, it was at that birthday party at Mr. and Mrs. Foye's Tremont Street home in May 1956? My mind travels to four months later, the diamond, and five months later, the wedding, then the honeymoon in Bermuda.

Since then we said to each other that we were blessed with one of those unique, compatible marriages. When we set our goals for our marriage, your comment was that there had never been a marriage of Midge Banks and Freddie Thomas on earth before, so God and we were in full control of this union.

I recall the ninth of each month, the surprising gifts you carefully selected with love. I think about the many nights you brought people home at crazy hours. Some of them were older, some young, some dirty, some clean, some slow learners, some degreed, some white, some black, some politicians, some non-voters, some poor, some financially successful, some religious, some atheist/ Jews/Catholics/Protestants, each searching for TRUTH through their respective leadership or fellowship positions.

Remember the college lectures to thousands of students across this country and in Bermuda, Puerto Rico, Paris, and London? Remember how some of the funds were collected from friends who financed some of the trips to help you? How about the many international guests we hosted in our Skuse Street home?

Anyway, I think you already know what's been happening since your death on February 24, 1974. Your friends witnessed a memorial service for you in the University of Rochester Interfaith Chapel on March 1, 1974. Roxbury Medical Technical Science Library is named in your memory. A proposal was submitted to City Council (Rochester) for 700 North Street Center to name this Center in your name. I have been asked to give permission to submit your name for consideration for the newly built Number 9 School.

My greatest interest is, of course, the development of the Freddie Thomas Foundation. Well, through God's guidance and truly dedicated friends, the Freddie Thomas Foundation purchased the Jewish Young Men and Women's Association Building at 400 Andrews Street from the Jewish Community Center of Greater Rochester. We have named this building Triangle Community Center.

Today, Columbus Day, we are laying the cornerstone in the entrance of the building. The plaque reads: "The Freddie Thomas Foundation and Triangle Community Center 1974." Behind this cornerstone is our time capsule you may review. In these archives are records of our objectives to carry out the philosophy of Freddie Thomas. Your crematory remains are also placed beside this capsule behind the cornerstone. In the capsule are writings from many Rochester Community Service organizations. This capsule will be sealed up for many, many years. It is my wish to be cremated and placed beside you behind this cornerstone also. We can always stay together in the Triangle Community Center.

I must tell you that without the dedicated volunteer service, first from John M. Griffin, along with Bessie Stallworth, Shelby Garfield, Bob Clarke, Art Hamilton, Eugene Parrs, Helen and Charles Corley, Jack Frank, Frank Holley, Mother and Dad, Mat Griffin, Terri Miller, The Jewish Community Center of Greater Rochester, Mae Hendricks, Foye Jones, City and County representatives, and many others not mentioned in this letter, our dreams would still be a dream. I think you woke us up to deal with REALITY.

Did you know that 52 brothers from Nigeria have come to live in the Triangle Community Center for a while? And that Ron Griffin is working on your books and research papers for the Freddie Thomas Universal Research Library? We cataloged over 5,400 books from your collection. I gave some of the medical and science books to your Medical Science Library in Roxbury, Mass.

Please, please continually send your spirit in prayers to all of us who are working very hard carrying our precious philosophy laid out by you.

Freddie, I'm married to The Freddie Thomas Foundation now, and it still has me hooked on YOU, but I love and thrive on it each minute of the day and night.

Love,

Midge

The Triangle Community Center

News of the renovated Triangle Community Center (TCC) and its willingness to assist nonprofit organizations traveled quickly, and Midge was no longer the lone occupant in the building. The dorm-style bedrooms were occupied, the classrooms were filled with teachers and students, and the recreation spaces were finally in use. It was the beginning of 1975, and the TCC started servicing over 200 organizations by offering them a space to hold their meetings and activities. The TCC offered their space at a fraction of the cost of other recreational facilities due to the financial subsidies provided by the Freddie Thomas Foundation (FTF). The amount provided by the FTF depended upon the need of the individual group, with some organizations benefiting from a full scholarship. The TCC was a self-supported operation, funded strictly from donations, and virtually all of the building's staff were volunteers.

Due to the sheer size of the building, many different organizations were able to take advantage of long-term leases, and Midge always seemed to have room for anyone looking for short- or long-term accommodations. One journalist from *The Rochester Patriot* perfectly described the building:

> From the outside, the Triangle Community Center looks like one more downtown behemoth from another era, probably half-occupied and threatened with demolition any day now. Inside, though, it's like a layer cake of Rochester's demography. Senior citizens, Cuban refugees, high school students, social service workers, and aspiring rock stars all claim their piece of the wedge-shaped red brick building at 380 Andrews Street – but there's always room for more.

"Room by room, the philosophy of Freddie Thomas, or Dr. Thomas or Professor Thomas or Brother Freddie, as he is best remembered, is becoming a practiced reality," stated journalist Adolph Dupree in a 1980 article in *about...time* magazine. "There are starting-over rooms for Alternatives for Battered Women. Club rooms for Kappa Alpha Psi. Creative rooms for Upstage Productions. Spiritual rooms for the Spanish-speaking Methodist Church. Educational rooms for the Ralph Bunche Scholarship. Gym rooms and racquet ball rooms and swimming rooms and sauna rooms for the people from Xerox and Corpus Christi, Bausch and Lomb, and Threshold and Burroughs and Jehovah's Witness. And cooking and eating and dancing and sleeping rooms."

The fourth floor of the building became a haven for abused women through the Alternatives for Battered Women (ABW) program. Women who came to the ABW to escape abusive relationships were given special accommodations within the TCC to ensure their safety. Oftentimes, Midge was awoken in the middle of the night to provide a safe, private room for women who had fled their abusers. The TCC made special alterations to the building to ensure the safety of these women, including limited access to the fourth floor, extra door locks, and one-way glass on the hall doors to ensure no one could peer inside. Women were often secretly escorted into and out of the building through back and side doors.

The TCC hosted 50 Nigerian soldiers in 1976 for an extended period of six months as they pursued communications training in the United States. The group's original accommodations, a hotel a few blocks away, had greatly insulted the men by requesting that they enter and exit the premises solely from a rear loading dock so as not to "upset the other hotel guests." When Midge heard of their situation, she was more than willing to help the soldiers, and they moved in the next day. Each soldier was given a room and three meals a day, all funded by donations made to the FTF from the governor of Nigeria.

Classroom spaces made available to the community were instrumental in allowing access to education to the underprivileged. The School Without Walls (SWW), one of the oldest alternative schools in the country, which places emphasis on individual learning and development, set up classrooms on the third floor and took advantage of the building's recreation spaces. Students in grades K-12 made regular use of the Center's pool, racquetball courts, and gym. An added advantage of adding the SWW as tenants was the additional exposure of TCC's available facilities to the community. In an article in a 1978 edition of *about...time* magazine, Gary D. Miller, a recent pre-law graduate from The University of Rochester, and the Assistant Executive Director of the TCC, reported, "SWW will ease, but not solve, our financial problems. The primary benefit of having it here is that it deals with an intricate and important facet in each of our lives: our education. Because of it, we expect more cultural activities, more media exposure, and more traffic at TCC."

The books from Freddie's private collection of 5,000+ that once lined the shelves in his living room on Skuse Street were moved into a room on the seventh floor. Although the volumes were not available to the general public due to their rarity and sentimental value, special requests could be made to borrow materials. The collection was so impressive that a local newspaper reported:

Purchasing his first books as a boy in Norfolk, Virginia, from money earned from performing odd jobs, Brother Freddie continued his collection at Virginia State University, Albany Medical School, Wagner College, and the University of Rochester. More books were bought and used while he was a research technician at Kodak and as a researcher of radiation biology and biophysics at the University of Rochester. The books were valuable in supporting research for his internationally recognized Chamber and Perfusion System invention to isolate blood cells. Even during his courtship and marriage to the former Midge Banks, Brother Freddie found time to supplement his collection of books.

In addition to Freddie's private book collection, Midge collaborated with the Rochester Public Library to house a branch library within the TCC's walls, sponsored by the International Black Brotherhood Association.

Midge ensured that Freddie and his teachings were remembered during the ongoing events at the TCC. At one such event, a Rochester Town Meeting held on June 19,1976, Midge debuted a song written by Freddie titled "All Over Town." The song reiterated Freddie's love and hope for Rochester:

If I had a dollar
I'd spend it in the morning
I'd spend it in the evening.
I'd work with people who like my hometown.

If I had a business in Rochester Town,
I'd hire those people who live in this town.
I'd ask for money to upgrade our city
And build a new future all over this town.

Give me the power to make change in this town.
Peddling for merchants all over downtown.
I'd focus for fairness for all our people.
I'd forget about profits, I'd forget about status.
All over this town.

Now we have enough dollars and we do have the power,
We can change unemployment all in this town.
Even in our Rochester home town.

Oh give us the power for Rochester town.
We'll vote for leaders committed for our people.
We'll fight rights for children and seniors
All over our home town.

As a music lover, Midge looked forward to hosting concerts at the TCC, but the auditorium was in need of extensive renovations. A TCC volunteer stepped up to the challenge and provided his renovation services free of charge in order to bring music to downtown Rochester. One of the first groups to perform in the newly revamped space was the Rochester Philharmonic Orchestra. "The November 28 [1975] concert was performed to an overflow audience in the newly renovated auditorium," stated a local newspaper article from 1976. "Sponsored in conjunction with the Puerto Rican Arts and Cultural Center and the Triangle Community Center, the Philharmonic presented "The Best of Us," featuring Black mezzo-soprano Hilda Harris and Puerto Rican pianist Yvonne Figueroa and the Bottom of the Bucket But Dancers." Many called the concert a historical event for the city of Rochester.

Music and concerts filled the halls every day at the TCC, especially after The William Crimm Institute of Music became a tenant. Other artists who performed at the TCC included B.B. King, Millie Jackson, Benjamin Matthews, and Claudio Lindsay.

In May 1981, when a local chapter of the YWCA closed its well-populated residence hall, about 75 female residents were displaced and would have been homeless if not for the room availability and affordable rates at the TCC. A group representing the women, The Coalition to Save the Y, worked with Midge and John on a transition plan to get the women safely into dorms within the TCC, with each room costing $35 per week. "We will be very pleased and happy to have them," John reported to the *Democrat and Chronicle* in May 1981. "Basically, we do have space and we can accommodate them. That's what we're in the business to do."

Originally, the YWCA requested space to rehouse 20 of the displaced women, but the TCC made accommodations available for over twice that amount.

Secondary education groups also took advantage of the TCC. Spanish-speaking students seeking careers in healthcare were offered special classes to help achieve their nursing degrees due to the increasing Hispanic population in Rochester requiring care. Bryant & Stratton College also utilized the space for their degree and continuing-education programs, and Alfred University's College of Nursing taught a class of 84 students under eight faculty members.

Recreation, one of the TCC's pillars, became a large part of its community offering. Local companies Kodak and Xerox would face off on the basketball court, and the pool was available.

The TCC was a flurry of activity, exactly what Midge had envisioned. She and her team of volunteers coordinated the scheduling of all the nonprofit groups, which rooms they wanted to occupy, and the supplies needed for each group so that every guest's needs were accommodated. An example of a typical Saturday schedule at the TCC included:

- 8:30 a.m. – 2:30 p.m., Volunteer Administrative Services, TCC Office

- 9 a.m., Receptionist and ABW Security reports for duty, Entrance Desk

- 9 a.m. –12 noon, Rochester Philharmonic Orchestra Rehearsal, Auditorium

- 10 a.m. – 3 p.m., School Without Walls Redecorating, 3rd Floor

- 10 a.m. – 11:30 a.m., Bausch & Lomb Racquetball, TCC Courts

- 11 a.m. – 1 p.m., Public Defenders Basketball, Gym

- 1 p.m. – 4 p.m., YMCA Youth Service (CETA) Program, 1st & 2nd Floors

- 1 p.m. – 3 p.m., Howard University Mothers' Club Meeting, Room 203

- 1 p.m.– 4 p.m., VIS Preparation for Wedding Reception, Auditorium

- 2 p.m. – 4 p.m., Kodak/Xerox Basketball Game, Gym

- 2 p.m. – 5 p.m., Literacy Volunteer Tutoring Program, TCC Library

- 2 p.m. – 3 p.m., New York City Visitors TSC Tour, Entire Building

- 2 p.m. – 1 a.m., "Volunteer In Service" Admin Supervision, 1st – 4th Floors

- 5 p.m. – 7 p.m., Wilcox Family Counseling, Chapel

- 6 p.m. – 2 a.m., Rochester Combat Security Patrol, 1st –5th Floors

- 7 p.m. – 9 p.m., Blackfriars Theatre Rehearsal, Room 208

- 7 p.m. – 10 p.m., Mellow Madness Band Rehearsal, Room 110

- 7 p.m. – 11 p.m., Spanish 7th Day Adventist Family Night, Recreation Areas

- 7 p.m. – 12 midnight, Swimming Pool Party, Pool

- 8 p.m. – 12 midnight, Spanish Wedding Reception, Auditorium

Over 200 community service organizations and agencies were supported or subsidized by the FTF between 1974 and 1982, including Action for a Better Community, the Rochester Firefighters, Spanish-Speaking Methodist Church, Shiloh Baptist Center, Rebels Black Policemen, Catholic Family Center, and the Monroe County Library Extension. The building was also made available to private events and parties, and the revenue collected from those affairs went right back into funding the TCC and the FTF.

An article from 1976 recorded many of the TCC's first tenets and documented the following:

- The City's Recreation Bureau used the center's pool from May until the end of October as a replacement for the closed Natatorium. The City now plans to train Triangle personnel to operate the pool and conduct swimming and safety courses.

- The auditorium has been the scene of the Miss Lilac Beauty Pageant and the Institute of Cultural Affairs' Town Meeting '76, as well as many dances, banquets, and concerts.

- Monroe County Legal Assistance Corp. has a conference room.

- The U.S. Department of Labor and the International Association of Firefighters maintain an office for the local recruitment of minorities into the Fire Bureau.

- Mildred Johnson, who for years ran the Virginia Wilson Helping Hand Center, now has an office there.
- The Public Defender's Office basketball team uses the gym for practice games.
- Mae Hendrick, on sabbatical leave from Xerox, organizes the volunteers and program activities.
- The Civil Service Employees Association has an office there.
- Dr. Virginia Walker provides youth counseling in "Virginia's Studio."
- A drop-in lounge and boutique has been set up by the staff for the "Retired Citizens of Leisure."

A sample list of organizations that utilized the TCC facilities includes:

- Alternatives for Battered Women, 12/1978 – 12/1981
- Action for a Better Community, 4/1981 – 12/1981
- Afghanistan Refugees, 12/1980
- Alfred University, School of Nursing, 2/1975 – 8/1977
- Artist Writers Guild*, 11/1976 – 3/1977
- Better Life Crusade, 10/1974 – 6/1975
- Blackfriars (Drama)*, 7/1977 – 10/1978
- Blackmate, 4/1981 – 12/1981
- Black Policemen, 12/1974 – 6/1977
- Black United Fund*, 4/1977 – 10/1977
- Catholic Family Services, 4/1981 – 12/1981
- CETA (Public Employees)*, 3/1978 – 3/1979

- Chapel, All Faith*, 10/1974 – 12/1981
- Christian Brothers Ministry*, 9/1979 – 12/1979
- Church, Full Gospel, 6/1979 – 12/1979
- City of Rochester, 4/1976 – 10/1976
- Contact of Rochester, 8/1976 – 7/1978
- Cuban Refugees, 4/1981 – 11/1981
- FZRA Lodge (Masonic), 12/1974 – 6/1975
- Free & Accepted Masons, 7/1975 – 7/1976
- Haitian Refugees, 7/1980 – 8/1980
- Inner City Sports*, 4/1975 – 8/1976
- Public Library*, 10/1974 – 12/1981
- Martin & Boylan (Aud.), 12/1978 – 12/1981
- Metropolitan Women's Network, 4/1980 – 12/1981
- Niazi Institute (School), 9/1975 – 7/1976
- Nigerian Army Sig. Corps, 4/1976 – 11/1976
- Noah's Arc (Music Group)*, 3/1977 – 11/1977
- Project Challenge, 7/1977 – 8/1978
- Ralph Bunche Scholarship, 3/1978 – 12/1980
- Rochester Firefighters, 7/1976 – 12/1976
- School Without Walls, 7/1978 – 12/1981
- Veterans Outreach, 10/1977 – 8/1979
- Veterans Outreach, Walker Counseling, 12/1974 – 7/1981
- Veterans Outreach, Wilson Helping Hand*, 10/1976 – 11/1978

*indicates fully subsidized by The Freddie Thomas Foundation

Along with the TCC facility, the FTF also provided financial assistance to community groups and not-for-profit organizations. Groups that financially benefited from the FTF in the late 1970s included:

- West African Cultural Night
- Haitian Support Cultural Party
- Funeral Receptions
- Narcotics Anonymous Support
- Beyond Racism Seminar
- Youth Enrichment Fashion Show
- Haitian Band Rehearsals
- Martin Luther King Memorial Service
- Youth Against Violence

After the TCC had been open for a few years, its army of volunteers had become professionals at managing the facility's events, which left Midge with some time to analyze the current state of her building and how it was serving the community. The building had become a place for non-profit groups to call home, but Midge wanted the building to help everyone, especially individuals who were alone and didn't have the comfort of being affiliated with a group.

Thinking back to her first home, where she and Freddie always had an extra place set at the dining table for anyone in need of a hot meal, Midge decided to offer meals at the TCC for those less fortunate. Through this drive to feed others, the WE CARE volunteer program was established in the early 1980s. One of the missions of WE CARE was to provide free holiday meals to anyone—both people living alone and large families—in need of a hot dinner on Thanksgiving and Christmas Day. The large auditorium space in the TCC gave Midge and her volunteers room to serve people as if they were back home in Midge and Freddie's dining room.

Dinners were presented on linen tablecloths, fresh floral centerpieces were arranged for ambiance, and volunteers dressed up in white uniforms. WE CARE volunteers took care of everything, from the food preparation and cooking to the serving and cleaning. A 1982 article from the *Times-Union* tallied that 300 people enjoyed Thanksgiving dinner at the TCC that year, an effort that required "300 pounds of turkey, 50 pounds of ham, 10 gallons each of corn, string beans, peas and beets, and dozens of pumpkin pies."

The WE CARE program initiatives extended beyond holiday dinners. The group made use of the vast space at the TCC and hosted programs such as New York State bingo games, sewing classes, children's programs, and senior Sunday dances.

People of all backgrounds used the building throughout the years, and one thing that always pleased Midge was that there were never any fights or violent altercations at the TCC. It was a safe haven in every sense of the word, a place where people could come, set aside their differences, and better themselves through education and recreation.

Although the TCC was thriving with activity, the financial weight and care of the building began to weigh on Midge. The TCC operated completely from private contributions and the rent collected from its tenants, and the staff was composed solely from volunteers. "For all these tenants and program activities, financing still remains a weak link in the Triangle" reported John Griffin in 1975. "More than brick and mortar support, financial support is being sought from the entire community for the service programs offered at the center."

A local publication reported on the TCC's financial troubles in the late 1970s, writing, "Because of a lack of working capital, underuse, and non-participation, the center remains just a brick building, and continues to operate at a deficit: currently $1,400 per month."

Heating the building during Rochester's bitter winter months was a huge expense, with an average utility bill of around $18,000 per month. The building's steam heating system was original to the building, and when Midge found out that it would cost over a million dollars to upgrade to a modern unit, she knew it was time to sell. As much as she wanted to keep the building, she knew she could still continue with the Freddie Thomas Foundation without a physical space. Plus, the money she'd be saving in utility expenses could be put toward more important community projects.

In late 1982, after eight years of ownership, Midge sold the property. She moved into an apartment in the building directly across the street on Liberty Pole Way so she could still be in close proximity to the building that had been the catalyst for the FTF. Throughout the years after the sale, she frequently ran into people who had benefited from the Center's offerings and always stopped to listen to their stories of how the building and the mission of the Foundation positively influenced their lives.

John Griffin and Midge pose with the TCC cornerstone, 1974.

NATIONAL ACHIEVEMENT AWARD
MRS. MARGARET "Midge" THOMAS

Mrs. Thomas was born in Rochester, New York. She is an Administrative Assistant at the Freddie Thomas Foundation, a charitable organization which she founded in 1974 in memory of her husband, to carry out his philosophy of "Helping People to Help Themselves". In September of 1974 The Freddie Thomas Foundation purchased the Jewish Community Center and renamed it the Triangle Community Center which has symbolized faith, hope and charity as it provided recreational, educational and cultural facilities for Blacks, Gentiles and Jews.

Since its inception, Mrs. Thomas has donated her services. She has provided stimulating and innovative worthwhile learning experiences within the center's environment. She has encouraged others to develop new skills while they acquired a depth in their old skills. She serves continually as a role model.

Midge earned a Jefferson Award for her achievements with the Freddie Thomas Foundation and the community contributions of the Triangle Community Center. The above is her National Achievement Award announcement from 1982.

Midge prepares a free holiday dinner with Congresswoman Louise Slaughter and her husband, Robert Slaughter.

Dr. Shirley Chisholm, the first Black woman elected to the US Congress, and the first Black candidate for a major-party nomination for president of the United States, visits Midge at TCC. They are attending the TCC International Soiree. The event was sponsored by the Rochester Club of the National Association of Negro Business and Professional Women's Clubs, Inc., which was later renamed The Rochester Genesee Valley of NANBPW Inc.

Chapter 4

The Miss Jane Pittman
Drinking Fountain

September 9, 2014

My Dear Freddie,

Freddie, it has been a long time (over forty years) and I still continue to be overwhelmed and inspired with the legacy you created. I cherish another opportunity to write a letter to you once again because when I write to you it's a powerful and meaningful therapy for me. Then I'm ok again.

This time, I'm recalling some of those seventeen precious years and two weeks of your life with me. I recall you teasing Dad and Mother to give you another Midge. Well, I have been looking for a clone of Freddie L. Thomas but I haven't found him yet, however, cherishing dearest memories of you are enough for me.

Honey, today is September 9, 2014, and every ninth of the month I still think about those monthly "I love you" cards with jewelry, perfume, lingerie, the small station wagon, formal gowns, and the mink coat. Fun stuff was surprise dates and the green and gold Chinese silk fabric, including a nine-inch zipper with matching thread, from your New York City trip and the Mother's Day trip to Denver to see my sister, Helen, because we were experiencing our desire to be with each other, etc.

Remember when we would shop at the Public Market on Saturdays and divide fruits and vegetables then deliver them to friends who had children? Oh yes, one time we laughed and talked to each other so much on one of our monthly trips that you missed an exit in Pennsylvania and we ended up in Princeton, New Jersey, and then we visited my cousins? Well, I could go on and on.

I specifically remember the day you talked about your dream to own the old downtown Jewish Community Center Building at 380 Andrews Street. Clearly, Freddie, you were still in our thoughts and actions when we made it happen after you left us by establishing the Freddie Thomas Foundation. Our archives are testimonies of the celebration when we installed FTF's cornerstone and renamed this building the Triangle Community Center on September 9, 1974.

And by the way, Freddie, I think it was you who inspired or suggested to LaShay Harris, Mr. (Rodney) Brown's secretary, that the book's title is *Silent Leader, The Biography of Dr. Freddie Thomas.* We know that you did not want pomp and circumstance over what truly came from your heart. We appreciate and thank you for all you did by reaching out to each of us and sharing your generous, unselfish wisdom. Freddie, you were a blessing to many of us. I believe and anticipate by reading *Silent Leader* that many will continue to be inspired to greatness by being a blessing to others.

Love,

Midge

The Miss Jane Pittman Drinking Fountain

One morning in 1985, Midge awoke feeling very sick. She had known she was coming down with a bug for a few days, but she chalked it up to the common cold. This morning, however, she couldn't ignore the chills and body aches that were accompanying her congestion. She went to see her primary care physician, who diagnosed her with the flu and sent her home with a bottle of medication and the directive to rest.

Midge struggled with fatigue on her walk home and felt so terrible that she knew she had to stop and take one of her pills immediately. Still a few blocks from her apartment, she entered a local restaurant and asked for a glass of water.

The waitress behind the counter was not at all accommodating to Midge's simple request and made her feel like a second-class citizen for even asking. Midge asked again and explained that she was sick and needed water in order to take her medication. The woman, who made a point to show her annoyance through a demeaning tone, told Midge that she could only have a glass of water if she paid ten cents. Midge was outraged but sucked in her pride and paid the waitress. She needed to take her medicine immediately and did not have the physical strength to argue with the woman.

Midge thought about the negative interaction on her walk home and replayed the incident in her mind for days afterward. The fact that a person could be denied a sip of water enraged her, and she vowed to do something to ensure that no one in Rochester would have to go through the same humiliation she had just experienced.

Although Midge followed the doctor's orders and rested a few weeks to recover from her flu, her mind raced with ways to make clean drinking water available to anyone in Rochester. She came to the conclusion that a public drinking fountain would answer the need, and she decided to approach the FTF board members with her idea.

Midge added her drinking-fountain idea to the next FTF meeting agenda following her recovery and shared her negative experience at the restaurant with the board members. The board unanimously agreed that a public drinking fountain was a worthy cause and sorely needed in the downtown area. While the idea of providing fresh water to downtown residents was strong in itself, the board members wanted to use this opportunity to have the fountain symbolize something deeper. Midge's story of being denied water was reminiscent of the segregated drinking fountains that existed prior to the Civil Rights Act of 1964, and her experience was a reminder that discrimination was still a struggle for the Black community.

One committee member, Rob Mendel, remarked that Midge's experience at the restaurant reminded him of a similar situation from the book *The Autobiography of Miss Jane Pittman*, a 1971 novel by Ernest J. Gaines. The historical fiction piece followed the life of former slave Jane Pittman and her life after she was freed. At the end of her life, at age 110, Jane Pittman drinks from a Whites-only fountain in an act of defiance.

It was this act that inspired the FTF committee to officially name the fountain the Miss Jane Pittman Drinking Fountain. The board thought the name was appropriate because, "In its flow it represents activity and progress. In its clarity it represents foresight. In its purity it represents goodwill."

Gaines was invited to be an honorary committee member and was active throughout the planning process, even taking time off from his writer-in-residence position at the University of Southern Louisiana to participate in fundraising efforts. A well-established author of novels and short stories, he was awarded a handful of literary awards for his work throughout his lifetime. He was particularly touched by the Foundation's recognition of his work, stating, "I've been given many awards all over the world . . . but never before a fountain."

In July 1988, Midge and her committee members worked with Rochester's Downtown Development Corporation (RDDC) to discuss the fountain's design and location. Everyone agreed that the fountain would be prominently displayed at Liberty Pole Plaza, a few short blocks away from the former Triangle Community Center. The location was chosen for its proximity to where Midge was denied water the year before, for its history of liberty demonstrations throughout the years, and because the location had been a symbol for humanity, liberty, and equality since the early 1800s.

The task of choosing a design for the fountain proved to be more difficult. With help from the RDDC, a series of designs were chosen and presented to the committee. Ultimately, a beautiful, three-spicket, American-made, forest-green brass fountain was selected as the winning design. This particular fountain would cost $10,000 to produce and deliver to Rochester, so the committee set to work planning fundraisers to offset the cost for the new Rochester landmark.

The committee's main fundraising event was the extravagant Lilac Festival Gala, held on May 19, 1989. Tickets were sold to the public, and people from all over the city attended to support the Foundation's lofty $10,000 goal. A replica of the fountain was prominently displayed, made from clay and donated by local art teacher Calvin Hubbard, and Gaines was in attendance to help champion the Jane Pittman moniker. Toward the end of the event, Rochester's mayor Thomas Ryan and county executive Thomas Frey delivered a joint proclamation: "We encourage all residents to drink from the water fountain and remember the principles represented in the character of Miss Jane Pittman."

The fountain arrived from California on July 26, 1989, and was installed in its permanent home at Liberty Pole Plaza three days before the official dedication ceremony. Although the fountain had not been formally introduced to the public, it was up and working, already providing water to the community. Eager to see the fountain in place, Midge checked on the installation process one afternoon while passing through the plaza. She was overwhelmed by a sense of accomplishment and satisfaction when she rounded the corner and saw the fountain finally in place, a culmination of over two years of fundraising and avocation. While there, she witnessed a policeman, some skateboarders, and a blind woman with her seeing-eye dog all drinking from and benefiting from the community fountain. At first she was taken aback because she had wanted to wait until the official dedication ceremony before the fountain was put into use, but she quickly changed her tune. The sight of people freely getting a sip of water when they needed it made her realize that she did not need to wait for a fancy dedication ceremony in order for the fountain to provide a much-needed service to the community.

On her way home, as she neared her apartment, she passed her neighbor working on his vintage 1957 Rolls-Royce. The car was stunning. She approached her neighbor, told him about the upcoming unveiling ceremony for the fountain, and asked if he would act as her chauffeur. He agreed without hesitation. At two p.m. on July 30, 1989, Midge arrived at the unveiling ceremony in that magnificent car, dressed in a bright pink suit to match the ceremonial bright pink fabric that was draped over the fountain to shield it from the public's view.

The event was hosted by Rochester Mayor Thomas Ryan (Rochester's 63rd Mayor, 1974 – 1994) and there were over 7,000 people in attendance. Remarks and speeches were made from various people who contributed to the project over the years, including:

- Iris Banister, Program Chairperson
- Mayor Thomas P. Ryan Jr.
- Ernest Gaines, Author
- Robert Mendel, Miss Jane Pittman Fountain Committee
- Midge Thomas, President, The Freddie Thomas Foundation

+ Helen Corley, Board of Directors, The Freddie Thomas Foundation

After a verbal dedication given by Mayor Ryan, Midge removed the pink covering to reveal the three-headed beauty. The committee had assigned a symbolic meaning to each of the three spickets: one spicket represented humanity, one represented liberty, and the last one represented equality. Midge chose those three areas to symbolize what America stood for. Mayor Thomas Ryan commented on this symbolism during his dedication speech and remarked, "This beautiful addition to downtown Rochester will be enjoyed by everyone for years to come. Thank you for the 'Miss Jane Pittman Drinking Fountain,' a visible symbol of 'humanity, liberty, and equality.'"

A song was written by Phyllis Wallace from the City School District to commemorate the occasion:

We care about humanity, liberty, equality, too
But most of all community
We care about each of you
This fountain reflects our need to help
Any outstretched hand
The water's flow is love that goes
From us to our fellow man

The man who most inspires us
Is alive within our souls
His body is no longer here
But his spirit ever grows
To reach to you and make you feel

His presence ever near
Brother Freddie, we salute today, we know that you are here

Let's take the time to thank some friends
Who made our dream to be
WVOR especially Bill Klein
Calvin Hubbard and Sibley's
Vargo Printing, Canopy, Together Wolfe Publications, too
Flower City Printing and Channel 31
Rochester Telephone, we thank you

We can't forget Ernest Gaines
Great author as you see
It's through his thoughts and transferred word
Miss Jane Pittman came to be
So reflective of our strive to gain
Our place in all communities
With humanity, liberty, and true equality

Mayor Thomas Ryan, hats off to you
And Midge Thomas, thank you
The Downtown Development Corporation and Downtown
Coalition too
We've worked together hand in hand
In love and harmony
The Jane Pittman Fountain and Liberty Pole
Symbols love and unity

Midge, Gaines, and Ryan took the ceremonial first sips from the fountain during the ceremony, and the community was invited up afterwards. At the end of the ceremony, the mayor officially named July 30, 1989, as "Miss Jane Pittman Day" in recognition of the fictional character who inspired the name of Rochester's new landmark.

The impact of the fountain went beyond providing fresh drinking water. The Rochester City School District developed a curriculum using *The Autobiography of Miss Jane Pittman* as a tool for teaching about the Civil Rights movement, starting in the fall of 1989. Peter McWalters, Superintendent of Schools, wrote to Midge and said, "On behalf of the district, I approve the project's request to involve students and schools so that the 'humanity-liberty-equality' message of the fountain can be brought to our children."

A few weeks following the dedication ceremony, Mayor Ryan sent Midge a heartfelt note thanking her for her efforts in bringing the fountain to Rochester. He wrote:

> I commend and thank you for your vision, dedication, and commitment which were all instrumental in making this celebration a success. We hope that you took justifiable pride in the crowds thronging Main Street, the exciting activities along the way and the unique new amenities that are now permanent features of Downtown's new look. The fountain is a testament to your own perseverance and community concern. . . . Thanks to your cooperation and support, Downtown Rochester's potential has never been brighter.

Members of the Miss Jane Pittman Drinking Fountain Committee; (seated l-r) Kathy Gillman, Beverly Davis, Betty Marion Anderson, Tracey Cleveland, and Betty Stewart; (standing) Robert Mandell, Midge Thomas, Paula Smith, Sylvia Paul, Lou Freedman, Beverly Lindzy, and Helen Corley.

July-30-1989

Freddie Thomas Foundation donates
Miss Jane Pittman Public Drinking Fountain
·Earnest Gaines, Author speaks on July 30, 1998

Howard Coles , stands as Midge Thomas speaks

Miss Jane Pittman Public Drinking Fountain Unveiling Ceremony
July 30, 1989 Midge Thomas, Founder
speaks of her experience of a need for Rochester
to have a public drinking fountain in downtown

Fountain ceremony attracts over 7000 citizens to Liberty Pole Plaza.
Record indicates it was the largest gathering of the "Main Event"

Above three pages of photos, taken from Midge's personal scrapbook, commemorate the "Main Event," which unveiled the new drinking fountain to the community. Midge is shown with fountain committee members Mayor Tom Ryan, author Ernest Gaines, and Rocester community members.

A new plaque was installed at the fountain's site in the summer of 2018. It reads:

The fountain is symbolic of the period in American history when Blacks and Whites had separate public drinking fountains. This era was portrayed in the Earnest Gaines novel, The Autobiography of Miss Jane Pittman. The three heads of the fountain represent equality, humanity, and liberty. The fountain fulfills a need, provides a convenience, and is a service to Rochester residents and visitors alike. Donated July 30, 1989, by the Freddie Thomas Foundation.

Midge, at age 96, visits the fountain (2022, photo by Karlie Lanni).

Chapter 5

The Triangle Square Center

September 27, 1978

Dear Freddie,

Today, Sept. 27, 1978, is the fourth-year anniversary of the Freddie Thomas Foundation and the Triangle Community Center. A few of us have been volunteering and pouring life into this precious downtown building daily on the average of 15 – 16 hours and 7 days a week. It has been pleasurable and rewarding working towards making our ideas and ideals work that we know you taught us before your departure.

Freddie, I have found myself working for this cause and I really haven't taken time to channel efforts for a fulfillment for myself. It's OK. I'm speaking of the companionship we highly shared together during our daily activities. I finally concluded to facing the reality of it all and accept the fact that I have enough fabulous and beautiful memories to cure all these inner emotional situations.

Love,

Midge

The Triangle Square Center

With the installation of the Miss Jane Pittman Drinking Fountain complete, Midge was able to focus on her next project, a new community space to fill the void of the Triangle Community Center (TCC) that closed its doors in 1982. Midge had never intended to sell the seven-story facility, especially after only eight years of ownership, but her hand was forced by the ever-increasing cost of maintenance and the need for a new, expensive heating system looming in the future. Although the building had been a behemoth to run and maintain, the service it provided made it invaluable to the community, and Midge longed to provide a similar facility once again.

Freddie had facilitated her search for the TCC from beyond, having expressed interest in buying the building before his untimely death. This time the search fell solely on Midge's shoulders, a challenge that excited her. She had learned a lot from managing the building at 400 Andrews Street and drew from her experience as her search for a new community space began.

The original building's enormous size was what first drew Freddie in and allowed the Freddie Thomas Foundation (FTF) to open its doors to a vast number of community members and events. But the expense and upkeep of such a massive property was a burden that Midge wanted to avoid this time around. A smaller space would also operate with fewer volunteers and resources, which would allow the FTF to focus on its mission of strengthening community initiatives.

A building located at 1180 East Main Street was available and checked a number of Midge's boxes for a desirable property. It was one story, moderately sized, and broken out into a series of rooms big enough to accommodate large parties and events, but small enough to maintain. Instead of purchasing the building this time around, the FTF decided to rent the space with an option to buy it down the road should they remain interested. The FTF set to work on renovating the meeting rooms and bathrooms, a task that was familiar to them given the elbow grease put into 400 Andrews Street only a few years earlier.

After careful consideration of a few names, the FTF's board decided that the new property would be called The Triangle Square Center (TSC).

Like the TCC, the new TSC needed many renovations in order for it to be an adequate meeting facility for the community. These renovations would be funded by donations and grants. In late 1995, the FTF received a grant of $20,000 from the Davenport-Hatch Foundation, a private foundation that provided support to non-profit groups in Rochester. Midge wrote her thanks to Mrs. Helen H. Heller, the Davenport-Hatch Foundation's secretary, and noted, "This certainly will improve our facility that we provide to other not-for-profit organizations and individuals in our community. We invite you to come see what we are about and what your contribution means to us. I appreciate your support and again thank you and your board for including us in your philanthropic services. It is our blessing to have persons like you to be able to provide special areas of need in our community."

One evening in the midst of the renovation process, Midge attended a Bingo Night at a local church with a few girlfriends. The time away from the FTF and its responsibilities was a needed break, as renovation costs had begun to mount and the responsibilities of managing the project's budget was becoming exhausting. With her cards splayed in front of her, and a dot marker in hand, Midge looked around the large crowd and started to calculate how much revenue the church was bringing in from this single event. And, more importantly, people were out socializing and enjoying the company of friends on a random weekday evening. If the FTF could host a similar bingo night, Midge thought, the revenue would help fund the renovations of the new TSC, and it could start serving the community.

Midge set to work buying supplies for the first TSC fundraising bingo game. Bingo daubers, cards, cage, and balls were sourced from a local gaming supply store on Goodman Street, and a room in the new TSC was completed in time to host the players. One of Midge's good friends, Zilla Higgs, sold homemade sandwiches and coffee, and other friends and Foundation members volunteered to help with the event.

The first bingo night was a huge success. People came with friends and partners, and people who came by themselves made fast friends with the people they were seated next to. Enough money was raised during that first event to convince the FTF to continue the games on a regular basis, and Friday Night Bingo became a regular occurrence for the next five years.

The weekly bingo games provided a steady source of revenue that facilitated the completion of the TSC's renovations and introduced the bingo players to its available facilities. Local community groups began to bombard Midge with requests to rent out the new space, a situation she welcomed because it meant that her latest project vision had finally come to fruition.

The people who approached Midge regarding renting space at the TSC were always thankful that such a venue had opened in the heart of the city. Such a facility was sorely needed to accommodate nonprofit organizations with small budgets and to welcome groups that were turned away from other locations.

One such group, AIDS Rochester, Inc., reached out to Midge, not to ask about reserving a room at the TSC but, instead, to ask about renting the bingo equipment to help facilitate fundraising events. "We are constantly looking for new and innovative ways in which to increase awareness of issues related to HIV/AIDS and to raise money," wrote Associate Director of Development and Communications Britton Lui in an inquiry letter in 1997. "Since the Lesbian and Gay community has been so supportive of our agency since its inception, we thought it might be appropriate to reciprocate their support by offering 'Gay Bingo' to the Rochester Community. It is very similar to regular Bingo except 'way more fun!' Gay Bingo has proven to attract members of all ethnicities, religions, and sexual orientations. We here at AIDS Rochester are very interested in further cultivating a relationship with The Freddie Thomas Foundation."

Midge and the Foundation had no problem with renting out their supplies and viewed this type of charity as an extension of the Community Center's services.

The Haitian Cultural Organization of Rochester (HCOR) was a regular group that used the TSC for a variety of activities. President Elie Nozier introduced himself to Midge, writing, "We are a nonprofit organization that helps people voluntarily, especially Haitian, in the Rochester community. We are a cultural, artistic organization that has been established since June of 1995." He worked with Midge on arranging spaces for HCOR band practices, an office space, and Haitian/American Nights that celebrated the Haitian culture with music, food, and dancing.

The TSC also provided a room for a monthly event hosted by Narcotics Anonymous. Chairperson for Activities Robert Lee contacted Midge in January 1997. "We are the Activities Sub-Committee of Narcotics Anonymous, our purpose is to plan activities for our fellowship, to help recovering addicts have fun while not using drugs," he wrote. Midge was more than happy to accommodate the requests of groups whose mission was to improve the lives of others for it fell within the mission of the FTF.

One offering at the TSC that particularly excited Midge was the after-school programs that were open to local school children. The classes and events gave kids a safe, productive place to spend their afternoons and reminded Midge of the tutoring opportunities she and Freddie had made available in their living room. Options from a 1997 TSC brochure included:

- Speaking Platform: Prepares youth for public speaking and jobs that require strong presentation skills.
- Black History Through Storytelling: Teaches children about African American history, Freddie Thomas, and other local leaders within the African American community.

- Book Club: Children develop cognitive and analytical skills while having fun.
- Writer's Club: Encourages free thinking while developing language skills and creativity.
- Movie Time and Discussions: Provides entertainment while allowing youth to interact with their peers and adults.
- Game Room: Flat out fun! To participate, all homework must be done, GPA of C or better is required, must have good school attendance and character discipline.

A number of small churches used the TSC's space for their worship services. It was an affordable location for small church groups that were without a formal space, and it was not unusual to host up to four different church services at once.

Along with allowing outside groups to use their space, the FTF hosted its own annual calendar of events and invited the public to take part in a variety of activities. The event calendar in 1996 included:

- January: Martin Luther King Luncheon
- February: Black History Art Exhibit & Program, Dr. Freddie Thomas Learning Center Birthday Program
- March: Alcoholic & Drug Rehab Counseling
- April: Camp Good Days and Freddie Thomas Foundation Easter Egg Hunt
- May: Lilac Tree Planting and Lilac Parade
- June: Community Service Job Training Programs
- July: Founder's Day Senior Luncheon

- August: *Baptized In Love*, a play by Camile Fadia
- September: Midge Thomas Birthday Fundraiser
- October: Children's Halloween Party
- November: Free Thanksgiving Day Dinner
- December: Free Children's Christmas Toy Party, 50 Christmas Baskets to Needy Families

The WE CARE volunteer organization, which had once relied so heavily on the original TCC, now had a new dedicated space in which to prepare and distribute their holiday dinners. The organization also happily utilized the space for new volunteer initiatives, including:

- Triangle Square Business & Professional Club
- Triangle Square Employment Training Program
- Triangle Square Youth Enrichment Program
- Freddie Thomas Leadership Institute
- FTF Computer Technology Program

Between the annual holiday dinners and other volunteer opportunities, WE CARE volunteers dedicated over 8,000 hours to community projects in 1997, with Midge volunteering 2,504 hours alone.

In 1998, through the weekly bingo games, donations, and space rentals, the FTF earned enough money to purchase the building at 1180 East Main Street. Unfortunately, permanent ownership was not in the FTF's future, as a number of major repairs, such as a new roof, were desperately needed. Learning from experience, the FTF's board members were hesitant to take ownership of another old building with an ongoing list of repairs.

In addition to the repairs needed to the building, Midge knew that she needed more time to take care of herself. Being incredibly active for 72 years had started to take a toll on her knees, and a double knee replacement with a long period of rest was in her immediate future. Although she was sad to see the TSC close its doors, she knew that the work of the FTF did not need a physical building in order to be successful. Ever a creative visionary, Midge had many more projects on the horizon.

Margaret Thomas, president of the Freddie Thomas Foundation, in one of the rooms ine building at 1180 E. Main St. where the foundation will move its headquarters next month. About 3,000 square feet on the first floor will be a bingo hall for nonprofit groups.

It's 3,000 square feet plus bingo
Foundation offering hall in new headquarters

By Jill A. Zelickson
Staff writer

Bingo fans will soon have a new place to go.

A bingo hall will open next month at the new headquarters of the Frie Thomas Foundation on East Main Street.

The foundation will move into a 26,000-square-foot, two-story building at 1180 E. Main St. in late April, said Margaret Thomas, co-founder and presiden.

About 3,000 square feet of the first floor will be reserved as a bingo hall for games sponsored by nonprofit agencies, she said.

The foundation will provide the space as a public service, Thomas said. It will charge only enough rent to cover expenses and subsidize the cost to organizations that can't pay.

There will be games sponsored by various organizations on Thursday through Sunday. The first game is scheduled for April 28.

The foundation, now at 147 Liberty Pole Way, has a lease with an option to buy on the East Main Street building, Thomas said. She did not disclose the price.

The rest of the building will house foundation offices, a kitchen, community events, and offices for businesses and other nonprofit agencies.

Thomas said that for some nonprofit organizations weekly bingo games are a major source of revenue.

"For some organizations it's the only fund-raiser," she said. "It's on a weekly basis and it sort of builds up. It's important to the organizations. ... It also provides a service to those people who do play bingo."

There are 100 bingo sessions a week in Monroe County sponsored by various organizations, said Dan Plonka of Greece, publisher of *Bingo Caller Magazine*, a monthly magazine listing bingo sessions in Monroe and six surrounding counti.

The magazine also runs a free bingo hot li paid for by its advertisers, listing the wee games. The number is 723-5155.

If about 150 to 200 people attend a sessi Plonka said, an organization can make a profit about $800 to $1,200.

The largest bingo site in the area is The Bin Palace, which opened last September at 341 Ridge Road, Irondequoit, in the Ridge-Sen Plaza. It has 10,000 square feet, separate roo for smokers and nonsmokers, and holds m sessions a week.

A bingo session, Plonka said, usually inclu 11 to 22 games. By state law, admission is $1 session. Paper books of games are sold for pri ranging from 25 cents to $1.

"The largest single prize you're allowed to g out is $250. Everybody has at least one $ game." he said. □

The local newspaper, the Democrat and Chronicle, announces the new space at 1180 E. Main Street (March 26, 1994).

Freddie Thomas Foundation
"WE CARE" Volunteers
serves Persons living alone and large families hot dinners
on linen table cloths, floral center pieces in white uniforms
on Thanksgiving and Christmas day for
over 30 years in Greater Rochester Community

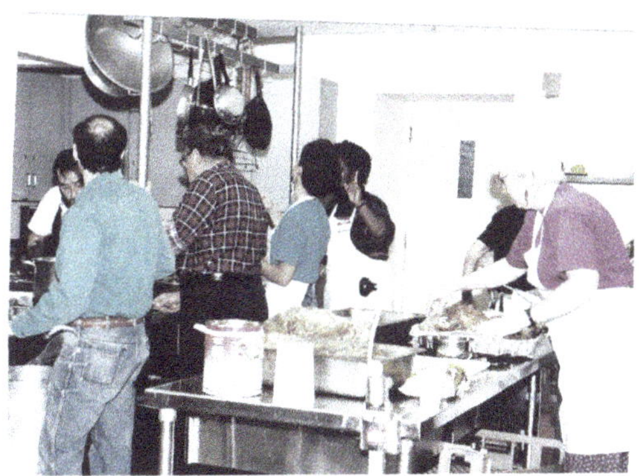

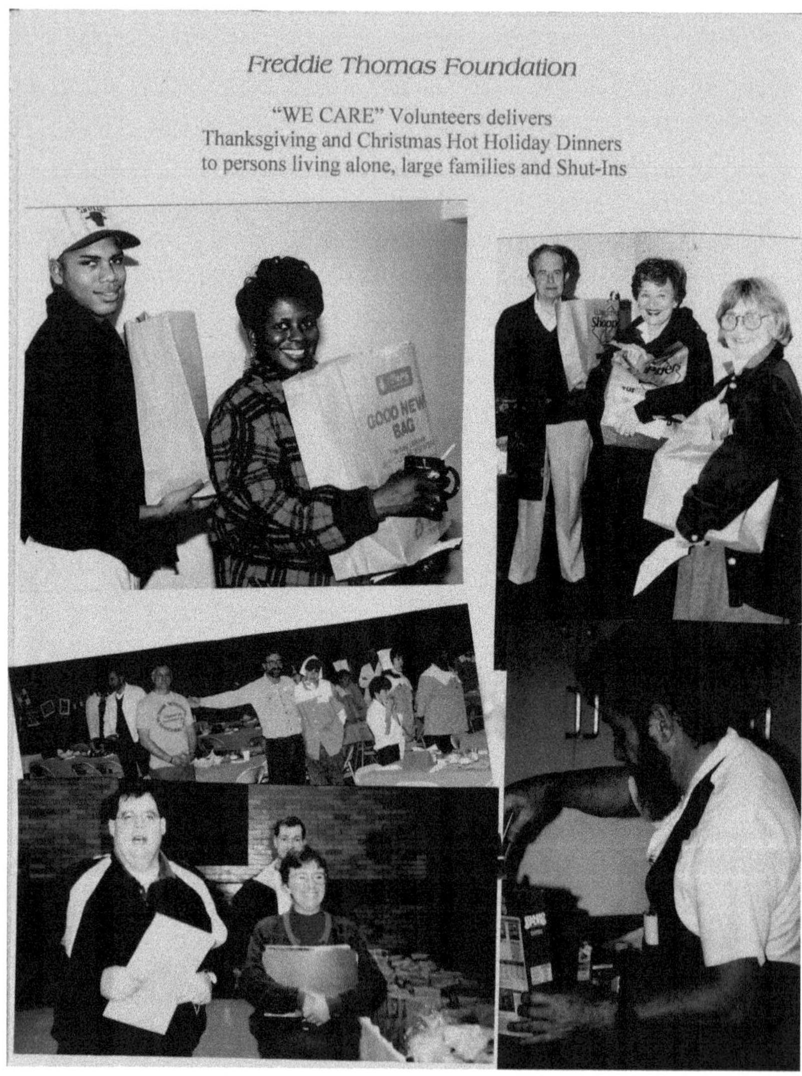

Above two pages of photos, taken from Midge's personal scrapbook, showcase WE CARE volunteers prepping holiday meals for distribution.

Chapter 6

The Dr. Freddie Thomas Learning Center

May 1995

Dear Freddie,

Another chance to share with you an important happening here in Rochester. I know you would approve of it.

There is a new school being built in the northeast area on Scio Street corner of Central Park. The 30-million dollar school is designed and planned by area residents, the City School District, Board of Education, and city officials. I received a letter from Loretta Johnson that the Board of Education has approved that the official name of this school be named in your honor and be called the Dr. Freddie Thomas Learning Center.

There was a community contest for a name, and over 100 entries were submitted. Your name was presented by Ruth McCray of Lyndhurst Street, which was the winner.

I read in a news article that this is the second public school in the country and first in Rochester whose policy has a voluntary dress code, which is black pants or skirts and white shirts or blouses. This is also what you wore most of the time. The school also has many community agencies involved within its operation. Lewis Street Center programs are a part of the structure of the north area of the building.

I am interested and plan to help the staff to assist wherever I can to motivate students in your school.

Until next time.

Love,

Midge

The Dr. Freddie Thomas Learning Center

In April 1995, Midge received a surprise phone call from a Rochester City School District representative. A new middle school was being erected in northeast Rochester at 625 Scio Street, and it was to be named the Dr. Freddie Thomas Learning Center (FTLC). Midge was pleasantly shocked. In the 21 years since his passing, she had spent so much time and energy preserving and honoring Freddie's memory. To receive a phone call out of the blue honoring him with an entire school was almost overwhelming.

As Freddie's widow, Midge was invited to give a speech at the official school-naming ceremony and reception on May 4, 1995, at the Rochester City School District Central Administrative Office building. The invitation came from Interim Superintendent Loretta D. Johnson, whose personalized note read:

> On behalf of the members of the Rochester Board of Education, it is with great pleasure that we acknowledge the choice of "The Freddie Thomas Learning Center" as the name of our new northeast middle school. The legacy of Dr. Thomas as a Black scholar, scientist, inventor, biologist, and humanitarian is one to be preserved and emulated.
>
> The selection process followed to choose this name in honor of your husband was a collaborative one which included strong community involvement. The Vision for the new school is one that also provides a distinct community focus with the promise and goal of "meeting the ongoing social, health, economic, and educational needs of all people who want to learn." Together with

our partners at the Lewis Street Center, we will work to make this vision become a reality at the "Freddie Thomas Learning Center."

New York State Congresswoman Louise Slaughter wrote a congratulatory letter to Midge, stating, "I am thrilled that the school district chose to name the school in honor of your husband. Dr. Thomas gave so much of himself to the Rochester community. It is only appropriate that his memory is preserved through the institution of education. Congratulations on this wonderful recognition!"

The first official school year welcomed its first class of 700 students in the fall of 1995, and Midge quickly became a familiar figure in the school's hallways. Being around the young students reminded her of the dining room classroom she and Freddie had once taught from 40 years earlier.

Midge and the Freddie Thomas Foundation's board of directors embraced the school's mission and proudly supported the school in the following areas:

+ Beautified the school grounds through landscaping projects

+ Recruited qualified mentors for students

+ Provided awards for students' achievements

+ Maintained the school's two display cases

+ Supported parent participation in projects and programs

+ Recruited motivational speakers

+ Identified a FTLC staff member to serve on the FTF board of directors

When the need for an official school song arose, Midge suggested that words be put to an original tune composed by Freddie. The school's students set to work composing lyrics to the original melody, and the genuine collaboration inspired students for generations.

School Song: "Dreams Do Come True"

Freddie Thomas is our hero

Dare to dream about your future

Freddie Thomas is our hero

In our hearts we have a picture

It's a picture of building hopes and dreams

And making them come true

It's all up to you,

They will come true!

If you trust and just have faith

In who you are

You can travel up the road

And become a star.

Good work and good plans

Will see you through.

It's all up to you,

Dreams do come true!

Original music by Dr. Freddie Thomas
Lyrics composed by students of Dr. Freddie Thomas Learning
Center
Musical Arrangement by Darryl Cathey

Dr. Freddie Thomas Week, an annual, week-long enrichment program centered around Freddie's birthday in February, was an idea proposed by Midge and eagerly accepted by the school's administrators. Each day of the weeklong celebration focused on a different theme, all with education and personal betterment at its core.

Monday of Dr. Freddie Thomas Week always focused on Freddie and his teachings and legacy, with the rest of the week dedicated to different themes to expose the children to careers and professionals they might not have access to on an average basis.

A sample schedule from the 2016/2017 school year included:

- Monday: Dr. Freddie Thomas Day, learn about his contributions to society
- Tuesday: Science Day, indoor rocket demonstrations and science experiments
- Wednesday: Board of Education members
- Thursday: Health and Wellness coach lectures. Rochester Mayor Lovely Warren presents and visits classrooms
- Friday: Lectures by Firefighters and American Red Cross heroes

At the conclusion of the first Freddie Thomas Week, Midge invited the students to the Triangle Square Center for a dual celebration to toast the successful week and to honor Black History Month. Students, parents, and teachers celebrated with step-dancing, poetry readings, and speeches and feasted on hotdogs, potato salad, tacos, chips, and donuts. The evening concluded with a birthday cake to remember the late doctor's birthday.

Another important initiative that Midge implemented with the Learning Center was the Ambassador Program, which was created to encourage children to prioritize their studies and to reinforce the benefits of a strong education with their parents. The more time Midge spent at the school, the more she became familiar with the students and their attendance habits. It was obvious when certain students did not care about their education and disrespected their own potential by skipping a class or school altogether. She approached the principal with an idea to help realign the children and their family's priorities.

The Ambassador Program was a group of about 15 adults Midge recruited to help with this community outreach project. The mentors Midge chose had similar beliefs in the importance of education and a willingness to reach out and connect with others. The group had a grassroots-style approach to connecting with children and their parents by asking around for students' addresses then going to their homes, knocking on their doors, and personally talking to them.

This volunteer work was not for the faint-hearted, for the Ambassadors faced many difficult home situations during their visits. The majority of visits were paid to single Black mothers whose resources and time were already stretched trying to maintain a household while keeping a job. Regardless, the Ambassadors persevered and visited as many families as possible, ever optimistic.

By 2007, the Ambassador Program had grown to about 40 volunteers, and their mentorship contributed to a 100 percent graduation rate for the 2006/2007 school year. Principal Sandra Jordan reported to the *Democrat and Chronicle*, "Last year, we graduated

100 percent of our students . . . we have 55 this year. We're going to have 55 walk across the stage."

In 2015, a biography of Freddie was published, and Midge made sure to donate copies to the school's library. It was important for her that every student had access to *Silent Leader, The Biography of Dr. Freddie L. Thomas,* by Rodney Brown, in order for them to fully understand the extent of her husband's contributions and why the school was named in his honor.

The Rochester community was devastated on September 10, 2002, by the sudden death of beloved police officer Allen T. Smith, who died in a motorcycle accident. Officer Smith's latest post had been at the FTLC, and the tragedy left the school community feeling a terrible loss.

Around this same time, Midge walked past the school one afternoon and was dissatisfied to find a dead pine tree flanking the entrance to the building. She was already thinking about initiating a beautification project, and dedicating a garden to the fallen officer who had kept the students safe seemed natural. In some way, having his name on a memorial garden would make it seem as if Officer Smith was extending his watch upon the students from above.

Midge set to work finding volunteers to help her initiate the Memorial Garden project, but ultimately, she spearheaded the majority of the work herself. She contacted Cornell Cooperative Extension to perform research on the environment's space, area, and soil. Steve Friedman, a landscape architect, was contracted to design the garden, which was to be in front of the school, and countless volunteers dug, planted, and watered until the garden was complete.

The Officer Allen Smith Memorial Garden was dedicated in a formal ceremony on September 10, 2003, almost exactly a year after his passing. The small dead pine tree was replaced by 18 large trees, including dogwoods, maples, lilacs, and flowing crabs, and shrubs and flowering perennials added a welcome rainbow of color to the entrance to the building.

Officer Smith's widow, Wandah Smith, attended the ceremony and remarked, "It's been the worst year of our lives . . . I am truly honored by this show of appreciation for Allen."

An article recounting the event in The Democrat and Chronicle stated, "The Rochester Police Department's Honor Guard performed with dozens of police in attendance. Chief Robert Duffy presented a plaque from Mayor William A. Johnson Jr. who declared Sept. 10, 2003, as a 'Day to Remember Allen T. Smith.'"

In special recognition of the Memorial Garden's 10-year anniversary, Midge, in partnership with her friend Gordan "Lee" Griffin and her ballroom dance group, Dance Lovers, donated a bench to the space. The bench was made from a natural granite rock dated to be about two billion years old and discovered in Penfield, New York. The bench was named "The Reflection Rock" by the school's principal, Miriam Cruz-Vazquez.

Police officers donated flowers to the Officer Allen Smith Memorial Garden in 2010

The Dr. Freddie Thomas Learning Center (2003) memorial garden

Chapter 7

Retirement Projects

∿

February 10, 2018

Dear Freddie,

These are just ten updates since the last time:

- It's February 10, 2018, and I can't believe we are celebrating your 100th birthday. Your legacy has been interesting and a mystery to us.

- Many times our friends get together to share memories of your wisdom. We met this year on February 24th for your 44th year transition.

- The Rochester City School District made a decision to change the permanent name of Dr. Freddie Thomas High School to Dr. Freddie Thomas Campus.

- Every year since the Dr. Freddie Thomas Learning Center opened in 1995, the teachers and I invite motivational speakers to celebrate Dr. Freddie Thomas Week.

- In 2014 I was interviewed by Rodney Brown for a story about the school. The story inspired him to write the book *Silent Leader, The Biography of Dr. Freddie Thomas*. The story tells of your childhood, education, employment, marriage, mentoring, health issues, wisdom, etc.

- Your name is listed in the 1984 edition of history of *4 score and 4 Rochester portraits,* by Joseph W. Barnes. These are 84 persons featured who were important to Rochester's history.

- The City Hall Black Heritage Committee selected 150 African Americans who made major contributions to Rochester. Your name is on this permanent "Ancestry Tree" plaque located in the City Hall entrance.

- Herb Hamlet is making copies of some of your lectures for us. He is adding a "Dr. Freddie Thomas Legacy" Facebook page on the internet.

- I have a display at the entrance of my apartment of about 43 recognitions of national or local achievement awards I have received since you left.

- I am volunteering in a few groups and spending more "me time" and working on several 1,000-piece puzzles as one of my new hobbies.

- I was awarded the Dr. Freddie Thomas Lifetime Achievement Award by the Gamma Iota Boule Foundation Recognition Program.

MT in Love

Retirement Projects

When Midge turned 75, many of her friends and former colleagues were slowing down and settling into retirement. But as her friends adjusted to this new chapter of their lives, she observed that many of them suffered from social isolation. A regular schedule of work and volunteerism provided a reason to leave the house and socialize each day. As glamorous as retirement seemed, a few friends confided in her that retirement left them feeling a lack of purpose and cut off from their community.

It was 2001, and as a widow for 27 years, she knew how easily loneliness could consume someone without frequent social engagements to reconnect with others. Her love of music and dancing filled her with wonderful memories of engaging with people, and Midge began to brainstorm ways to develop an open ballroom-dance forum for the community.

Together with friends Gail Parello, Steve Lagergren, Della Mosca, and Roderick Thomson, Midge founded Dance Lovers in October 2001 in response to this social need. For a location, long-time friend Reverend Mike Lubas opened his parish, the Lutheran Reformation Church at 111 North Chestnut Street. And for instruction, Midge tapped into local ballroom dance instructors who were eager to exhibit their dancing skills and offer instruction to an interested audience.

The first Dance Lovers party took place on a snowy Saturday night, a perfect opportunity to lure people out of the hibernation of their homes to partake in an evening of socialization. Over 200 people braved the winter elements and packed into the Lutheran

Reformation recreation room to let loose dancing the cha-cha, mambo, foxtrot, swing, jive, and salsa. Women wore long gowns and men donned suits and tuxedos. The flyers that were distributed to advertise the event specified that no dance partners were needed, and single dancers were paired with other available guests upon arrival. Attendee Kathy Houston from Marion, New York, remembered, "I often came alone . . . [but] I always had partners to dance with. I loved it because Dance Lovers always had gracious hosts and hostesses."

From 7 p.m. to 11 p.m., guests danced, mingled, and enjoyed light refreshments, all while Midge observed approvingly.

Dance Lovers parties became a regular event after the first party's success, taking place the third Saturday of every month. Parties often had themes such as April in Paris, October Masquerade Ball, and December Holiday Festival Ball, with suggested attire to match the theme. As the events became more popular, additional event locations were included to allow people from all over the Rochester area to attend. Locations included The Reformation Church, Iniklori Studio, River's Edge Party House, and the Arthur Murray Dance Studio.

Dance Lovers stopped hosting parties in 2013 after 12 years of connecting people through dance and music. Although the events were no longer a staple on people's calendars, the friendships that were solidified through Midge's initiative continued off the ballroom floor and will be forever cherished.

Music and dancing had been a resounding theme throughout Midge's life. Dance Lovers had provided her with a consistent musical engagement once every month, and she missed the regular social opportunity it provided. At 90 years old, she was still blessed with sharp hearing and coordination, so she decided to create a new event at her home to celebrate music and friendship.

Midge's neighborhood summer jazz concerts began as a spontaneous jam session consisting of a few friends improvising outside Midge's apartment on Liberty Pole Way, but they quickly grew into weekly events that hosted full bands and crowds of people spilling off the sidewalks into the streets. The Just Us Jazz Jams, as they became known, were located in the busy Downtown district, and neighbors in adjoining apartment buildings would open their windows to let in the cool summer air and listen to the free music playing down below. Always a planner and a hostess, Midge would prepare for each evening concert by setting out folding chairs for the audience, laying out snacks and refreshments on her patio table, and calling friends to remind them of the evening's festivities to ensure a good turnout.

Rip Winkle & The Van Drivers Band were regular performers at the Just Us Jams. Paul Ruske, the group's drummer, loved the spontaneous feel of the outdoor concerts and recounted, "Each of our musicians always enjoy your refreshments, friendliness and hospitality, an evening of fun with your guests. Sometimes personnel may change but we prefer not to rehearse. We appreciate this opportunity for you helping us."

Members of the audience were always encouraged to bring instruments and join in or take the microphone and lead the group with a song or two. It didn't matter how much talent someone had, or how inexperienced they were singing in front of a group, all were welcome to perform and partake in the night's festivities.

Midge had lived in her apartment on Liberty Pole Way, directly across from the former Triangle Community Center building, since the TCC closed its doors in 1982. The TCC building was now called The Harrow East Athletic Club, and after renovations, it offered gymnasiums, an indoor track, a fieldhouse, pickleball leagues, and group exercise classes. But alterations to the building across the street were not the only changes Midge observed from her window. She noticed that the condition of her street and its character seemed to be deteriorating with time. Street signs were broken and faded, uncollected trash piled up in the gutters, and the overall lack of charm did not match the charisma of its residents.

Midge founded the Liberty Pole Way Improvement Project in the summer of 2022 to draw attention to the repairs her street needed and to attract volunteers to help with the cause. She launched a letter-writing campaign to local businesses and institutions, explaining the project's mission and requesting donations to the cause from local businesses. She partnered with Downtown ROCs! (Rochester), a non-profit organization that supports projects that add to the vibrancy and beauty of Downtown Rochester.

"I wanted to let you know that I have decided to formalize my downtown revitalization efforts by officially registering Downtown

ROCs! as a 501(c)(3) non-profit organization," founder Mike Gilbert wrote to Midge. "I am excited about this big step because it might open the door to more opportunities to impact the neighborhood and the downtown area overall. . . . I would respectfully invite you to be a charter Board member of Downtown ROCs! You have been an inspiration for me and I would be honored if you would accept this invitation."

With Midge's determination behind the cause, and her newfound status as a Downtown ROCs! board member, many small upgrades to Liberty Pole Way were completed within a few short months: two benches, a wastebasket, and two large flower planters were installed, damaged traffic signs were replaced, sidewalk bricks were repaired, the grids around two trees were repaired, and the Flaum parking lot was repaired and painted. Future plans for the project include repairs to the handicapped parking spaces, additional flower planters, new parking signs, light pole banners designating the area, and a donated metal art sculpture.

Date	Theme	Optional Attire
Jan 15	10th Anniversary Crystal Ball **Rivers Edge Party House @ 31 Paul Rd. Rochester, NY	Blue/Silver
Feb 19	Young At Heart Dance Party	Red/Pink
Mar 19	St. Patty's Dance Party	Green/White
Apr 16	April In Paris Dance Party	High Fashion
May 21	Purple Passion Dance Party	Purple Shades
Jun 18	Black & White Ball	Black/White
Jul 16	Red-White & Blue Dance Party	Red/White & Blue
Aug 20	Summer Sizzle Dance Party	Optional
Sep 17	50's Rock & Roll Dance Party	50's & 60's
Oct 15	Masquerade Ball	Optional Masque
Nov 19	Harvest Moon Dance Party	After 5 Fashion
Dec 17	Holiday Celebration Ball	Glitzy/Sparkly

No Partner Necessary

Light
Refreshments
served 7 till 10:30

Information

Gail: 746-3290

Midge: 325-3873

A Dance Lovers flier from 2011 announcing the themes for the upcoming year.

Office of the Mayor
By these Presents, Greetings:

Whereas: Midge Thomas, along with John Griffin founded the Freddie L. Thomas Foundation in 1974, which serves as a memorial to her late husband Freddie L. Thomas, a distinguished scholar, educator, scientist and humanitarian ; and

Whereas: Midge Thomas' vision led the purchase of the Triangle Community Center at 380 Andrews Street, by the Freddie L. Thomas Foundation, where it hosted international guests, while providing numerous services to many others throughout the community, subsequently moving to 1180 East Main Street in 1994, where its name was changed to the Triangle Square Center; and

Whereas: Midge Thomas has actively supported organizations such as: the Zonta Club of Rochester, the American Red Cross, Negro Business and Professional Women's Club, Downtown Coalition, Toastmasters International, and AME Zion Church, among others, and has been the recipient of several awards, such as: the Jefferson Award, National Achievement Award, International Association of Negro Business and Professional Women's Club, Gannett News/Times Union "Club Woman of the Year", the Duke Ellington-First Church Divine "Hall of Fame", and a nominee for the Athena Chamber of Commerce award, to name just a few; and

Whereas: Midge Thomas was instrumental in organizing a committee to recognize an African American heroine named Ms. Jane Pittman, by arranging as a gift to the City of Rochester, the Ms. Jane Pittman Public Drinking Fountain at the Liberty Pole Plaza, where all who thirst can receive a free drink of water.

Now, Therefore, I, William A. Johnson, Jr., Mayor of the City of Rochester, do hereby proclaim September 28, 1996, on the eve of her birthday, to be

MIDGE THOMAS DAY

in Rochester, and urge all individuals to acknowledge the outstanding contributions of Midge Thomas to the Rochester community.

In Witness Whereof, I have hereunto set my hand on this 28th day of September in the year 1996.

Signed: *William A. Johnson Jr.*

Mayor, Rochester, New York

Rochester Mayor William A. Johnson's official declaration of "Midge Thomas Day," September 28, 1996.

Just Us Jazz Jam concert, Summer 2022

Chapter 8

Letters to Midge

Dear Midge,

Throughout your lifetime you've written thousands of letters. I've had the privilege of reading many of those letters during the past year as I've performed the research for your biography. Your letters advocated for those less fortunate, proposed new community projects both big and small, humbly accepted major awards, and thanked those who have collaborated with you throughout the years.

You saved and cherished hundreds of these letters in the plastic sleeves of your scrapbooks, but it was your heartfelt letters to Freddie that made me pause and realize that these words you shared with him should help build the structure of your biography. Although the words you wrote were originally intended to be between you and him, the raw emotion and positivity from each one helped tell the story of each chapter that followed. I thank you for allowing me to share those letters with the world.

It's now time for people to share their words with you, to tell you how you inspired them, provided friendship, and offered motivation over your lifetime. The letters that follow are from only a small handful of the people you've worked with and befriended over the years because, had I reached out to each and every person you've touched, this book would be never-ending!

Thank you for allowing me to tell your story,

Laura

July 5, 2022

Midge,

There are some people who leave a lasting impression on a person, and you are one of those people. When we first met I knew you were a person that I wanted to keep in my circle of women of wisdom.

Although we may not see each other on a regular basis, when we do connect it is one of my moments of being in awe.

I remember the first time we met, how humble you were. As I continued to say you are a legend, you just smiled and said – no, I am just Midge. You are more than just Midge! You are a woman who has carried on the legacy of your husband – Dr. Freddie Thomas. Without you, who would be there to tell his story? I was honored to serve as Principal at Montessori Academy at the Dr. Freddie Thomas Campus. What made these years so memorable was being able to celebrate the man with a woman who shined when we spoke about him. The first year of Dr. Freddie Thomas week was such a joy. The students embraced the week, learned about Dr. Freddie Thomas, and engaged in learning activities from so many of our community members. What was most honorable was the fact that you interacted with the children as though you had been a part of their schooling for years. You were there every day, you showed up and showed out! Yes, each day you were crowned Principal! This honor was bestowed upon you because of your dedication and commitment to the celebration of your husband, Dr. Freddie Thomas.

Each year of my service, we continued the week of celebrations, with a birthday cake at the end of the week.

Midge, I honor you as you have honored Dr. Freddie Thomas for so many years. Toni Morrison's "Song of Solomon" says, "when you know your name, you should hang on to it, for unless it is noted down and remembered, it will die when you do." Midge Thomas, your name is noted down and will be remembered!

Dr. Shirley JA Green

Former Principal, Montessori Academy at Dr. Freddie Thomas Campus

Commissioner of the Department of Recreation and Human Services –

City of Rochester

July 10, 2022

Dear Midge

Back in 1988, 34 years ago, I was a School Social Worker assigned to #5 School on Plymouth Ave. in the Rochester City School District.

In those days there was a special pre-school program named Twixt that was housed in the building. Your sister, Helen Corley, was an administrator in the Twixt program, and I had the good fortune to meet her in the course of my daily activities.

Midge, as you probably know, Helen approached me one day and asked if she could speak with me privately. Little did I realize at that moment that I was being recruited to offer my free time and energy on a very special project.

Helen went on to explain that she and her sister Midge Thomas had a vision of bringing a new resource to the City of Rochester that it desperately needed at that time.

What was needed was a drinking fountain that could be utilized by any citizen regardless of the color of their skin. Nobody would be denied a drink of water and nobody would have to pay for that drink.

Once I said yes to Helen, I was assigned to the Miss Jane Pittman Drinking Fountain Committee. This committee, working together with your We Care Committee, would be responsible to bring the vision of this wonderful new water source to reality.

As soon as I got involved I was inserviced as to the name of the drinking fountain. You wanted all of us to know the story.

Drawing inspiration from the book by Ernest Gaines in 1971, *The Autobiography of Miss Jane Pittman,* and the 1974 movie of the same name starring Cicely Tyson that told the story of a young Black girl that was denied access to a "white only" water fountain.

My involvement with this fountain committee and the We Care committee in pursuit of our fountain was a lifechanging experience for me.

First and foremost was my opportunity to meet you and experience knowing you and working with you. I was provided a "front row seat" to witness you working your "magic" in bringing people together to reach goals that needed cooperation and a shared belief in the value for everyone.

Midge, I also wanted you to know how much it meant to me to be asked to speak at the Community Dedication in Liberty Pole Plaza in front of that giant crowd and to speak at your father's funeral. You have always had faith in me and I will be eternally grateful.

All of us, thanks to you, were able to meet "like minded" people from completely different backgrounds and neighborhoods and form beautiful working relationships.

Midge, to this day, I have never wanted to lose touch with you. To stay in touch with you helps me to keep connected to the best parts of myself: my positive energy, my creative energy and my loving heart.

You have always inspired me to reach higher and believe in the goodness of people to join together to build new communities built on caring for each other.

With love and respect,

Rob Mendel

Original member of the Miss Jane Pittman Drinking Fountain Committee

July 11, 2022

Dear Midge,

Am so pleased and humbled that your author (Remembering God is your first author and Laura your most recent!) invited me to join others in writing a personal letter to you.

Hard to believe it was back around 1980 that we first met at what was the historic home (1868) of Reformation Lutheran Church, 33 Grove Street in downtown Rochester.

In the later 1980s, due to street renovation and alignments, the address of 33 Grove was replaced with 111 N. Chestnut. And while the historic building remains, the structure is now home to a vibrant Christian community called Glory House.

I mention this because you and I have had many conversations about life and its array of changes. Some changes are for good, some not, most having elements of both. Yet, all have a purpose and direction if we allow the eyes of faith, not merely the eyes of the world, to be the interpreter. And you, dear lady and friend, have been a shining example of using the eyes of faith, with savvy wisdom and vision for the sake of hope among community, government, education and just good old-fashioned one-to-one relationships.

You have kept the legacy and spirit of your husband, Dr. Freddie Thomas, alive among us here in Rochester and beyond. When in your wedding vows you said I do . . . you have!! Midge, you have the gift and grace for MAKING THINGS HAPPEN. Freddie must have sensed that from the git-go. And the community of Rochester, your family, friends, colleagues, associates and collaborators surely affirm it, notably in this special and heartfelt biography by Laura DiCaprio.

Finally, I want to conclude this letter with something a bit more personal. Midge, from the very first time we met, I felt in the presence of a gracious, intelligent, perceptive, "let's get it done" lady and soul . . . yet within all these, there lives a child-like spirit. You have this twinkle in your eye, in your aside comments, in your loving a good party, music and dance, in your wanting to believe the best in people and clapping your hands with joy when it all comes true.

May we all find the same child within ourselves, whatever "age" we live in or our personal time clocks. Your birth years are certainly respectable, Midge; your lifetime . . . is eternal. (Mark 10:15)

With continued prayers and love,

Mike & Sondra

Rev. Michael H. Lubas

Free Holiday Dinners Committee

July 12, 2022

Dear Midge,

My love for you grows deeper every time we get together. Our common thread is dancing, we met on the dance room floor over 25+ years ago, so many I can't remember exactly. We became fast friends and formed a dance party like no other in Rochester, NY. We got together with 4, 5, sometimes 6 or more individuals who had the same passion for dance. At our meetings we agreed upon the theme, the professional dance teachers who would give a lesson before the open dance, the dance hosts who would be available to dance with ladies who did not have a partner, the food and beverages, and of course, the music. We provided a clean, comfortable atmosphere where other dancers could feel safe and enjoy the love of dance. Many friendships developed, still today we keep in touch with the special bond that we created with other dancers. Our success became evident to us when dancers from Syracuse, Buffalo, and New York City came to our dances. It was a magical time. We transformed the place where we held our dance, each time according to the theme decided on. All of the women who participated dressed in ball gowns and high heels, and the men wore ties and dress pants. We all had an appreciation for the style of dance that was obvious in our flare and decoration. We dissolved the corporation after 16 years of Ballroom Dances, there was now a void, and to this day our friends tell us how much they enjoyed our dances.

You and I have what some people call synergy—we call it a higher intervention. We could tell one another what projects we were involved in, what we needed, and by the greater power it would happen. An example is when you needed a rock to display in front of The Freddie Thomas Learning Center, alas. I had a friend who had such a rock, a glacier rock, over centuries old that slid down during the ice age. It was donated and now sits in front of the building.

We've kept in touch on a regular basis, gotten together as often as possible. Your giggle that tickles your thoughts is a signature that no one can duplicate. I miss you if I don't see you. We inspire each other, we give each other fuel that burns the fire in our souls. We know what we have, we use it in positive ways, and our goodness rubs off on each other, so much that others want to be around us. We carry on as if it is a natural happening and we both know that we were brought together as a gift of God.

My hope is that everyone can find a spirit-friend like I have in you. When they do, treasures will abound, cherished memories will happen, they'll never stop believing, they'll have mutual respect for each other, and their love will forever grow.

Sincerely, Della Mosca

Dance Lovers, Friend

July 18, 2022

Dear Mother Thomas,

Thank you for being the amazing, phenomenal woman that you are!

Before I met you, I thought people just grew old, got sick, and died. Watching and experiencing "who you are" has changed my perspective on life itself.

It's not just what you do (although that's not to be overlooked) but it's "who you are." It's because of who you are that you can do what you do! I've witnessed and experienced your selfless love of God, people, and the community as you have favorably touched the lives of all those who encounter you—and that's amazing!

Your unselfish love shines through and through wherever you go, leaving people, places, and things better than when you found them.

"Who you are" is a unique and special brand that sets you apart, makes you stand out, and inspires me, and I'm sure others, to be the best that we can be. Your examples of selfless love show us that we shouldn't do anything out of selfish ambition or empty pride and that everything should be done with humility. We should consider others more important than ourselves, and we should look not only to our own interests but also to the interests of others.

You are a living testimony, an example of what living a life of selfless love produces. A long, fulfilling, and purposeful life!

Thank you for being "who you are."

Daughter Beverly

P.S. When I grow up, I want to be just like you!

July 26, 2022

Dear Midge,

We met October 21, 2001, and what a ride it has been! Your friendship has meant the world to me and together we created something beautiful with Dance Lovers. For twelve years every Saturday night we created a get-away fantasy. Community, friendship, companionship and unity all under the guise of dance.

Do you remember our first dance and all the excitement it provided? You and I stood on the sidelines and marveled at the happiness we witnessed and created. What a moment!! All the joy that was in that room. We never imagined the impact and the contribution we were making to the dance community.

Our efforts have never been duplicated because we gave our hearts and souls to this. To this day I can honestly say that timeframe will go down in my history as one of the most magical and enchanting times of my life. I suspect you share the same feelings.

You are an inspiration to all who know you, Midge, and you set a fine example to those around you. God Bless you always, my dear, and I'm so glad you came into my life.

Love you, girlfriend.

Love, Gail Parello

Dance Lovers

July 27, 2022

To My Dearly Beloved MWN Sister Margaret Midge Thomas,

It is with heartfelt gratitude that I have accepted this opportunity to pen an open letter to you as my friend and associate of more than four decades.

As I reflect upon some of my fondest memories of our relationship, there are several that stand out among them all.

First, at the time when we met, there was a need to provide a movement where Black women, especially, would have a forum to address some of the issues they faced. You were very instrumental in helping to achieve that goal by becoming a founding member of the Metropolitan Women's Network (a local section of the National Council of Negro Women, Inc.) that was chartered in March 1980. As a Founder and President (Emeritus) I relied upon your expertise, community contacts and philanthropy to assist in launching this new venture for the 150 women who initially joined representing various socio-economic groups. You added credibility to our numerous and varied programs and activities by providing offices and facilities in the Triangle Building for implementation of the programs and networking activities. Many of our programs empowered members and their families to gain greater access to resources, volunteer their services to others and advocate for women's rights. You even provided housing for Haitian Refugees who were involved in one of our programs offered at that site.

Secondly, my life was enriched professionally, as well as personally, after being introduced into your circle of friends and associates who represented many cultures and levels of society.

Finally, I wish to thank you for being a role model who has always been consistent in your purpose in life, which is to serve and embrace others regardless of race, ethnicity, social or economic standing, while also carrying on the legacy of your late husband, Dr. Freddie L. Thomas.

I pray that God will Bless you with continued long life, health, strength and prosperity and that you will keep your charming personality.

Your Dear Friend Forever,

Lilly Washington Haygood

Metro Women's Network (MWN)

July 29, 2022

To: Midge Thomas:

When I think about the influence you have had on me and my thinking over the years, I see your influence as a very positive factor in my pursuit of goals. You always pushed ahead on any project which you valued and then wanted to work on. Somehow, you handled all the possibilities that might get in the way of successful completion.

You continued to progress regardless of obstacles or delays that might cause others to stop unnecessarily. You looked for projects that benefited a wide range of people, operating with the idea that helping others was an over-riding goal. You operated with a "never give up" attitude if you thought the project was worthwhile.

All of these attitudes and approaches to goal setting were impressive. And I want to thank you for helping me learn how to better evaluate goals and then to pursue them with a realistic "Never Give Up" attitude.

I have known you for almost 35 years and have always been impressed with the variety of projects you have accomplished. It is difficult for me to sometimes connect them all because they were so varied and yet still of value to the community. And even today, when you are in your mid-90s, you just don't seem to stop. It is amazing and inspirational to me when I consider what you have done and what you still work on.

I see that, at any point in life, there is always more to do for ourselves and for others. I wish you could go on forever, but the lessons demonstrated in your life will certainly continue to positively help the lives of many others who have come to know or work with you.

Many thanks for all you have done and the lessons you have provided.

George Scharr

CEO, Flower City Group

September 19, 2022

Hi Midge,

Yesterday when I was cleaning out my closet I found some photos of the Miss Jane Pittman Public Drinking Fountain. I'm giving them to you.

I thought about the night, along with my two children, Lorraine and Paul, when I first met you at the war memorial in February 1987. I had just moved from London, England, to Rochester a few months after dealing with the death of my husband.

While we were attending this event, I became interested in The Freddie Thomas Foundation. This is when you were working to give downtown Rochester the drinking fountain.

Remember, my family volunteered to help to host a reception in our home for Earnest Gaines, who was the author of the autobiography of Miss Jane Pittman novel? We also helped you when you were working for several years with Bill Klein, film critic, annual Oscar Awards Reception and Party.

I loved your three boat-ride birthday parties which were so creative. Two of your parties were in my reception room.

For over thirty-five years our family still loves your celebrations and even this year in 2022 your weekly Friday Night Free Jazz Jam live music parties at your home.

Hilda, Friend

October 2022

Dear Ms. Thomas,

After our conversation last week, it was brought to my remembrance that my acquaintance with you was in 1977 when I married my first wife. The wedding was held in the Triangle Community Center auditorium at 380 Andrews Street. The ceremony was most memorable. We selected Triangle because we liked the classy architectural atmosphere.

I had the opportunity to support many positive projects you did but didn't realize you were the founder of The Freddie Thomas Foundation.

I have always been in awe of your commitment to supporting families, agencies, clubs, businesses, education, recreation, and the social community at large. Since 1974 you have continually set the stage for the future growth and development of our City of Rochester.

It is my honor to have had the experience with you for over forty years.

Sincerely,

Barry Jones

Owner and Broker, Anointed Realty

October 25, 2022

To Mrs. Midge Thomas,

A trailblazer, advisor, and a friend.

Faith Chapel Apostolic Church would like to say thank you for your service and consistent acts of kindness to the city of Rochester, NY. Your heart to help others has been a blessing to many near and far. From the beginning in working with your husband, the late Dr. Freddie Thomas, to the present time, seeds of hope and love are still blooming in a dying world.

You offered your resources and extended your hand to help our students thrive educationally by way of reading and writing, inspiring them to be the best that they can be.

As you've often said, "if you can perceive and believe your dream, you will achieve!"

We hope that this letter of our appreciation will encourage you in knowing that your work was never in vain.

May the Lord bless you, and keep you;

May the Lord make His face shine upon you, and be gracious unto you;

May the Lord lift up His countenance upon you, and give you peace.

With love,

Mrs. Millie M. White and Bishop Samuel White Jr.

Faith Chapel Apostolic Church

800 E. Ridge Road, Rochester, NY 14621

⟋

October 19, 2022

I met Midge about four years ago when I joined TOPS Club #180. TOPS is a National Association meaning "Take Off Pounds Sensibly."

She was very outgoing and friendly. Everyone treated her like a queen and listened to every word she said.

I thought, "who is this lady?" Well-spoken and well dressed. As time went on I learned that Midge was the wife of the late Dr. Freddie Thomas.

She is a community activist who did and still is doing a lot to improve our community.

As for myself and TOPS club ladies, Midge has always been a cheerleader with encouraging words or a motivational gift for me:

To reach my goal

Don't give up

Take baby steps

Stay positive

Slow and steady wins the race

Today is October 19, 2022, and Midge Thomas, thank you for being you!

Alison McCulough, Friend

October 2022

Mrs. Thomas,

I met you when I was 14 years old, and your husband Dr. Freddie Thomas invited me to your home where he would share with me about life, our culture, and being a good man. You would prepare snacks for me to enjoy. As time went on, I lost contact with Dr. Thomas but never forgot his teachings. Years later, I ran into you at Dr. Freddie Thomas Learning Center on Scio St. for a Black History Month celebration honoring Dr. Thomas. How excited I was to see you again. Our relationship began again that day.

I can never repay the kindness you both shared with me during my childhood. I was honored when you asked me to paint some little figurines for you and then you suggested I paint a mural on the wall of your dedicated conference room.

Dr. Thomas always told me to remember my dream; I dreamed to be an artist. Even though I didn't go to art school, I am a self-taught artist. My gift has taken me to many countries and cities. I share my art in a prophetic space through a ministry called Artistically Revealing the Spirit. My work has been shown in restaurants, libraries, churches, Jewish Synagogues, City Hall, and other prestigious places. In the spirit of giving back, I have dedicated my former years to sharing my love of art with the homeless population in a free creative arts space called Revelation Rochester located at St. Joseph's House of Hospitality, where I am also the Art Director. I desire to make the invisible visible through art. I guess in a way Dr. Thomas's spirit of giving and moving others to live better lives on through me.

It has also been a pleasure spending Friday evenings at your summer jazz nights outside your home. Your friendship has been appreciated. You are indeed a wonderful person and a wealth of knowledge to our community.

Sincerely,

Richmond Futch Jr., Artist

October 20, 2022

Hi Midge,

I met you as a TOPS 180 member about ten years ago and it's been a pleasure for me to know you. TOPS is a national program to help persons maintain, lose, or gain weight.

It is good to know that both of us share the same time of being in an organization that benefits us both physically and mentally.

Every Wednesday morning I look forward to picking you up at 8:45 with a thermos of hot coffee for me or we may share breakfast or lunch after our meetings all through the COVID-19.

Midge, you have lifted our spirits by including us in some of your creative social activities such as free Jazz Jam summer parties outside of your home, those dance parties at The River's Edge Party House, and those Harbor Town Bell Boat Cruises.

I cannot find the words to express the admiration I have about you sharing with me as a special friend and sister.

May God continue to bless you, and keep up the good work.

Sincerely,

Betty Galloway, Friend

October 21, 2022

Dear Midge,

Thinking back so many years ago, even before I met you, I remember reading an article in our local newspaper about a "Family of the Year." It was the Banks family and how committed they all were to improving our Rochester community. This of course was your beloved family, your parents and siblings Charles, George, Helen, and you.

Several years later I met all of you, except your deceased husband, Dr. Freddie Thomas, who was also a humanitarian committed to serving our community. You and your dear sister Helen almost immediately got me involved with opportunities to use my musical and artistic gifts. You hired me and my band to play for many Freddie Thomas Foundation events, women's groups, birthday parties at various clubs and restaurants. Many events were at the Freddie Thomas Foundation Triangle Square Center at 1180 East Main Street where I'd meet many prominent people of Rochester and other international dignitaries.

I remember a City Festival you started for several years where you gave me and my beloved artist friend, Sonya, a chance to do portrait drawings of people downtown on Main Street during the celebration. We did Dance Lover's nights where you invited talented friends opportunities to display their talents and services, which added a creative element, and many free Thanksgiving and Christmas dinners at the downtown Lutheran Church.

Most recently, playing outside your apartment on Liberty Pole Way Jazz Jams on Fridays all summer months are my highest pleasurable times. Thanks from each of our musicians.

It is such a pleasure to reminisce and recall all these things through the years of which I'll ever be grateful to you, Midge.

With love and admiration,

Tom Tosti, Friend

October 21, 2022

Dear Midge,

My name is Mary Lou Mees and I remember when you and Helen Corley visited a garden party off East Avenue in 1989 when a group of White and Black women met to discuss how we could help to bridge the gap of racial issues. Each of us were active, civic-minded women in our churches and community areas of interest.

Five of us met at the Top Of the Plaza restaurant and voted to create our name, The Grapevine. Our picture is just some of the members on page 91 in Betty Strasenburg's "My Life's Journey" book.

We met monthly for over 10 years and shared our dedicated efforts for integration and racial harmony.

Nancy Dean was founder of Sojourner House supporting single families and Wilson Commencement Park, a center for starting over for women in transition and needy families.

We were one of the major supporters in bringing Tops store to that neighborhood.

It's through efforts of Betty Strasenburg that the new Main Street Eastman School Auditorium is a reality.

Cathryn Carlson was the major contributor establishing the downtown East Main Street YMCA across from the Eastman Music School.

Rosa Wims was owner of Wims Community Center on Genesee Street corner and Sam Macree Way.

We supported Salvation Army Church and Social Services opening on Liberty Pole Way. You became a volunteer member of Salvation Army Women's Auxiliary.

I remember when you got your eight years volunteer award from the Margaret Strong Museum.

We designed a banner at Nancy Dean's home of "Community Women in Action" for participation in the 1995 Labor Day parade.

Tom and I volunteered for you for the Free Holiday Dinners at the Reformation Church on Chestnut Street and when you founded the Miss Jane Pittman Public Drinking Fountain.

Pearl Rugglass, who owned a beauty salon on Genesee Street, was awarded as founder of the Jamaican Organization of Rochester.

You and Gail Parello invited Tom and me to your Dance Lovers lessons on University Avenue.

You supported our William Warfield Scholarships concerts and opera singer Derrick Smith concerts.

The mission and the dedicated contributions of these "Women of Grapevine" is still active and worth their efforts to the Greater Rochester Community today.

-Mary Lou Mees, Member, Women of Grapevine

November 6, 2022

Dear Midge,

Thank you for our friendship and words of wisdom through the years. I remember when you sat on the Rochester American Red Cross Board of Directors. At that time the Red Cross was developing goals around diversity and inclusion. You were an important voice in helping the agency develop, recruit, and implement programs to reach these goals.

Midge, you have been gracious in sharing your knowledge and team spirit. As an African American woman, wife, and grandmother, I am humbled and amazed by your lasting and positive impact on not only the African American community but the Greater Rochester Community.

It was my honor to serve on The Freddie Thomas Foundation Board of Directors with you. That was where I witnessed how much this community means to you. Serving on The Freddie Thomas Foundation Board of Directors gave me the opportunity to work on projects that positively impacted the Greater Rochester Community. I was also able to further enhance my own personal knowledge.

Thank you, Midge, for your kindness, generosity, grace, and wisdom. I will continue to admire your generous spirit. When I want to volunteer, I will use the lessons I have learned from you to guide my volunteer efforts.

Midge, you have always had a special place in your heart for our children's education. Community service should be a goal for our children. I will encourage my grandson to follow your example to be the best person he can be through education, kindness, and service to others.

Love and Joy,

Patricia Marks, Friend and Dr. Freddie Thomas Board Member

November 2022

Dear Mother Thomas,

Good afternoon. I would like to talk about how I met Mrs. Thomas (Mrs. T). It started back in 1970. My wrestling coach and I were walking home from school, I was having trouble with math. He was going to introduce me to a man that could straighten all that out. This is my wrestling coach and I wanted him to like me, but I didn't necessarily believe what he was saying.

When we got to Mrs. Thomas's house, she was taking groceries out of the car and we helped her. She was and is a very lovely lady, very proper, prim, and pris. So, we went inside and Brother Roy introduced me to Brother Freddie. As I got to know Brother Freddie, I also got to know Mrs. T. What was amazing about her was how she treated Brother Freddie's friends. Her relationship with Brother Freddie was amazing. During that time she exemplified what a wife should be. I never heard her and Brother Freddie get into an argument. No matter which day you stopped at their house, if it was around dinner time, there was a plate for you. That's amazing because people do not operate that way today.

Because of her example I believe I was able or am able to be married as long as I have been, forty-five years and counting. I believe I have been married longer than any of my friends. Mrs. Thomas knew how to treat Brother Freddie, and Brother Freddie knew how to treat Mrs. Thomas.

Mrs. T exemplifies unconditional love for her husband. She has done so many things in her life to honor her husband and his "students," yes "STUDENTS." I am more than proud to say that I am a "student of Brother Freddie," a student of the Thomases. As the saying goes, "behind every great man is a great woman." Mrs. Thomas is that great woman. Just examine her accomplishments after the departure of Brother Freddie. The Triangle Community Center, Harold East and the naming of a school after Brother Freddie.

Mrs. T, whom I refer to as my "mother," has done tremendous things for me. She works with the mayors of Rochester for the betterment of the city. She coached me through my B.S. degree in Engineering from the University of Texas in Austin, through my MBA at Centenary College in Shreveport, Louisiana. Throughout my professional career she has been there. I headed up Public Work Departments, Infrastructure Division Manager in Abu Dhabi, Consultant in Africa and Saudi Arabia. When I need counseling, I could always go to Mrs. T as my "Mother."

Your "Son,"

Jerome Rogers

March 8, 2023,

Dear Mrs. Thomas,

I met you, wife of the late Dr. Freddie Thomas, in the lobby of the Sloan Performing Arts Center on campus at the University of Rochester.

As our conversation developed, we quickly became interested in learning more about each other that day, and shortly thereafter, you gave me your phone number and address. Telling me to feel free to call or visit, which I did. Three days later I was sitting at your kitchen table soaking up all of the incredible history that only you could explain and provide archival documentation of a lifelong creative visionary and activist in your own right.

What I love about you is your warm relatability, sharp wit, sense of humor, and wonderful laugh. When I'm in your presence, I can feel the joy of your laughter and I know that you care for my wellbeing in its totality, intellectually, and spiritually. You're always willing to bestow your wisdom. When I spend time at your table, I readily understand that you are mission-driven. You inspire me to continue the mission and embrace the legacy for change in our community.

Mission accepted with respect, love, adoration, and gratitude always,

Your new son,
Rashaad Parker

March 8, 2023

Dear Ms. Thomas,

Although we met under peculiar circumstances, I'm so glad that we did. The inspiring book about the life of Dr. Freddie Thomas informs the reader that he died nearly 50 years ago. Although some of your accomplishments since his passing are mentioned, I did know you were still with us.

When Mr. Rodney Brown introduced us a couple of weeks ago, my reaction was one of shock. It took a moment or two for me to gather myself in all the excitement. Since that moment you have been generous with your time, sharing more inspiring stories of your life with Dr. Thomas. The spirit of excellence, which animated your lives together, is still very strong.

We are blessed to have a living legend among us. Your mind is still sharp and your ability to inspire remains evident. Thank you for believing in all people no matter the circumstances, no matter the obstacles. I pray God give you many more years of active influence within our community.

Your Son,

Don Armstrong

꠹

March 10, 2023

Dear Midge,

We met in 1975 at the Triangle Community Center while taking karate class with The Purple Dragons. I saw you walking through the hallways seeing how things were going. I was able to see the different services the Center had to offer. There were rooms for those seeking shelter, an Olympic-sized swimming pool, a grand ballroom, and classrooms.

The next time I saw you was downtown, 34 years later. I got to know you better and understand your mission as God ordained her.

It was through you that I got to know your husband, Dr. Freddie Thomas. You do not seek attention but do as your heart tells you. I am blessed to be a part of your life's journey.

Mario Howell

City of Rochester

City Hall Room 308A, 30 Church Street
Rochester, New York 14614-1290
www.cityofrochester.gov

Malik D. Evans
Mayor

April 3, 2023

Margaret "Midge" Thomas
Rochester, NY, 14604

Dear Midge:

Please accept this letter of congratulations on the upcoming publication of your biography, "Letters to Freddie," by Laura DiCaprio. I can think of few people in Rochester more deserving of having their life chronicled in such a manner. This book will be a treasured gift for future generations of Rochesterians, especially those who seek to learn more about the people behind our history of civil rights and community advancement. You and your late husband, Dr. Freddie Thomas, have played a powerful role in that history.

Almost from the moment you and Dr. Thomas were married in 1957, you both became well known in Rochester for your tireless service to the community. Of course, as a renowned scholar, biologist, inventor, and researcher at the University of Rochester, Dr. Thomas achieved iconic status in Rochester's proud pantheon of Black leaders.

But since Dr. Thomas' passing in 1974, you have quietly etched your legacy into the story of Rochester's never-ending pursuit of equity, inclusion, and social justice. You founded and served as president of the Freddie Thomas Foundation; established the Freddie Thomas Scholarship Fund and the "We Care" initiative; co-founded the Rochester/Genesee Valley chapter of the National Association of Negro Business and Professional Women's Clubs (NANBPW); and served as president of the Zonta Club of Rochester. You have also provided valuable service through such boards and organizations as Alpha Psi Omega Sorority and Fraternity, the Women's Coalition of Downtown, and the Liberty Pole Way Improvement Project.

Your many awards and honors include the National Sojourner Truth Award; NANBPW's National Achievement Award; recognition by the National Women's Hall of Fame and the National Jefferson Award; and the Rochester Black Heritage Community Service Pioneer Award; and two Rochester Mayoral "Midge Thomas Day" proclamations. In 1987 you worked with Mayor Thomas P. Ryan Jr. to install the Miss Jane Pittman Public Drinking Fountain in Liberty Pole Plaza to ensure Downtown visitors would never have to pay for a drink of water.

Your contributions to Rochester have made our community a better place for everyone, especially those historically left behind. It gives me great pleasure to know the story of those contributions will live on in your biography.

Sincerely,

Malik D. Evans
Mayor

Midge and Mayor Malik Evans (2023)

Chapter 9

Legacy

May 1, 2023

Dearest Freddie,

This is my last letter I am writing to you because I never said to you before -"Thank You Freddie," for selecting me to be your wife. You really gave me a platform to find out who I am. It was God's design for my future. This direction lead me to at least fifty local as well as national recognitions or awards displayed at the entrance of my home. I thank each of those groups for honoring me as their awardee.

Each of my volunteer contributions and gifts were to meet the needs of the greater Rochester community and were done from the inspiration and memories of you Freddie.

I was interviewed in 2017 for a book about you, Silent Leader, The Biography of Dr. Freddie Thomas, written by Rodney Brown. Some of my projects are written in this book, Letters to Freddie, written by Laura DiCaprio. Imagine, we inspired her and Rodney to write their first books.

Thank you, Laura and Rodney, for dedicating your gifts for each reader to "pass our torch."

I love you Freddie, until we meet each other again.

Midge

Legacy

During the research phase of this book project, I met with Midge on Saturday mornings from January 2022 through April 2022. Every week, I would visit with her in her apartment, where she'd tell me stories from her past and hand off a packet of news clippings, letters, and awards for me to comb through and scan. She came prepared for our chats, and I came to each one eager to learn more about her amazing life.

What amused me was that our interviews were always accompanied by unexpected visitors to Midge's apartment. Midge is adored by so many in the Rochester community that friends and family members frequently stopped in unexpectedly to visit. These were welcome interruptions because I was able to meet so many wonderful people throughout this time, and each one had stories to share about how they met and knew the amazing Mrs. Thomas.

I brought my son Charlie to one of our interviews because I felt it was important that he meet Midge. She was welcoming, as always, and started asking him about school—what grade was he in, did he play an instrument, what were his favorite books.

As we sat around her small kitchen table, I realized that moments like this were what made Midge *Midge*. The way she easily understands people from only a few minutes of conversation and how people instantly connect with her is a unique life skill not many possess.

It is this ability that has enabled her to positively impact the lives of thousands of Rochesterians in her lifetime. After listening and understanding what people needed, she did whatever it took to provide for her community.

The people she has impacted are forever grateful. Teenagers and young adults she once mentored in the 1960s and 1970s still visit her for chats and advice, even though they are now in their sixties and seventies. She still refers to them as her sons and daughters, and they gratefully receive loving advice from their Mother Thomas.

At 96 years old, Midge still assesses the needs of Downtown Rochester and schemes up ways to improve life for herself and those around her. Whether it's through a letter writing campaign or connecting with people of influence from her past, Midge still has a way of making her voice heard.

Her advice to others who want to effect positive change on their communities includes:

- **Pray** and volunteer where you see the need.
- **Share** whatever you have been blessed with to uplift and help prevent social, economic, and cultural problems that exist today.
- **Give** while you have health and strength.
- **Leave** notable contributions for future generations to benefit from for years to come.

Dear God,

I am Margaret-Midge-Banks-Thomas.

You know who I am better than I know. About 97 years ago you created an ingredient for Milton and Ethel Banks to form life. Then you blessed them to name me Margaret Caroline. I was that little brown baby, born to help people.

All during my childhood life, I had these special thoughts and feelings that I was special, but I didn't understand or know why you chose me to be who I am.

My three near-death experiences proved how you brought me through so easily. After I grew up and left my parents, I met one to share my life with. You chose Freddie L. Thomas. I never knew why your plans for our union only lasted 17 years and then I would be back on my own again. I have pleasant memories of our marriage. Some are published by author Rodney Brown in his 2015 book *Silent Leader*.

I realized in my journey that I must obey all options you gave me. Therefore, I obeyed when I heard you utter "Create the Freddie Thomas Foundation, and I will be with you all the way. Buy that building at 380 Andrews Street in Rochester, NY. You must volunteer full time tirelessly and freely to provide the needs to many of my people."

Everything I did afterward was through you, for the Rochester community.

It was only through you, God, that these projects were so successful. Thank you for these 96 years!

Yes! I am Margaret-Midge-Banks-Thomas!

Margaret "Midge" Thomas

Chapter 10

Awards and Recognition

Career:

1947 – 1959, Owner, Orchid Beauty Salon

1963 – 1974, Owner, Original Creation Bridal Accessories

1974, Co-Founder, Freddie Thomas Foundation

1974 – 1982, Executive Director, Triangle Community Center

1982 – 1997, President, Freddie Thomas Foundation

1993 – 1998, Executive Director, Triangle Square Center

Professional and Community Involvement:

1958, Co-Founder of the Rochester Club, National Association Negro Business and Professional Women's Club, Inc.

1959 – 1992, Board Member, Ralph Bunche Scholarship

1974, Founder, Freddie Thomas Foundation

1974, Assistant Director, Triangle Community Center

1974 – 2007, Founder, The Dr. Freddie Thomas Scholarship Fund

1976 – 2022, Member, The Salvation Army Ladies Auxiliary

1981 – 1985, Member, Coalition for Downtown

1982 – 1997, Founder, Free Thanksgiving and Christmas Dinners

1983 – 1985, Member, Metropolitan Women's Network

1984, President, Freddie Thomas Foundation

1989, Founder, Miss Jane Pittman Public Drinking Fountain

1990 – 1992, Member, The Rochester Events Network

1990 – 1998, Volunteer, The American Red Cross, Rochester

1990 – 1996, Volunteer, Freddie Thomas Foundation

1991 – 1992, Member, Vision 2000

1994 – 1996, Member, Grantmakers Forum

1997, Founder, The Dr. Freddie Thomas Scholarship Fund

1999, Founder, The Dr. Freddie Thomas School Ambassadors Program

2001, Founder, The Liberty Pole Book Club

2001, Founder, The Liberty Pole Way Neighborhood Association

2001 – 2014, Co-Founder, Dance Lovers Ballroom Social Parties

2002, Founder, Officer Al Smith Memorial Garden at Dr. Freddie Thomas High School

2002, Consultant, DIVA Connections Journal Series

2007, Founder, The Dr. Freddie Thomas High School Ambassadors Program

2014, Founder, Free Friday Night Jazz Jam Social Evenings

2019, Charter Member, Downtown ROCs Board of Directors

2022, Founder, Liberty Pole Way Beautification Project

Awards and Recognition:

1969, Honorable Mention, Gannett Times Union Newspapers Club Women of the Year Award

1975, Business Award, Rochester Negro Business and Professional Women's Club

1982, Jefferson Award, American Institute of Public Affairs

1982, National Achievement Award, National Association of Negro and Business Professional Women's Club, Inc.

1982, Certificate of Appreciation, NYS Division for Youth Foster Parent

1990, Rochester Volunteer Award, Rochester Downtown Program Trust Fund

1991, Sojourner Truth Award, Rochester Genesee Valley National Association of Black Professional Women, Inc.

1991, Heart Award, Zonta Club of Rochester

1991, Women in Business Award, Rochester Chamber of Commerce

1994, ATHENA Award Nominee, Rochester Women Chamber of Commerce

1995, Woman of Greatness Award, Life Community Center

1996, Midge Thomas Day, Office of the Mayor, Rochester, New York

1996, Community Service Award, Omega Psi Phi Fraternity, Inc.

1997, Community Service Award, Dr. Freddie Thomas Learning Center

1998, Salute to Midge Thomas, Rochester City School Board of Education

1998, Black History Month Award, Rochester City School District

1999, The Dr. Freddie Thomas Learning Center Certificate of Recognition

2000, Senior Award, JCPenney/United Way Golden Rule Awards

2003, Inductee, National Women's Hall of Fame

2004, WE CARE Volunteer of the Year Award, Freddie Thomas Foundation

2006, Certificate of Appreciation, The Salvation Army, Rochester, New York

2008, Empowerment Award, National Council of Negro Women, Inc., Metropolitan Women's Network

2008, Sankova Award, Sankova Festival Organization

2009, Pioneer Honoree, City of Rochester's Black Heritage Committee

2009, Empowered Woman Award, The Rochester Genesee Valley Club

2010, Al-Haijah Sahirah Muhammad Aleem Exemplary Service Award, The International League of Muslim Women, Inc.

2011, "Love Never Gives Up" Recognition Award, Paradise Temple 1149

2011, Community Service Award, Rochester Above

2012, Recognition Award, Atlantic Union Conference of Seventh-Day Adventists

2014, Midge Thomas Day, Office of the Mayor, Rochester, New York

2018, Special Mayoral Recognition Certificate, Mayor Lovely A.

Warren

2022, Greater Rochester Martin Luther King Jr. Commission, Honored as an Elder by The 2022 Juneteenth Celebration Elder Tribute Committee

2023, Women's History Month Recognition, City of Rochester

Bibliography

Chapter 1; Becoming Midge Banks Thomas

Author Unknown. "Five Women Win Honors For Their Good Deeds." *The Times-Union* (Rochester, NY), October 21, 1969.

Brown, Rodney. *Silent Leader, The Biography of Dr. Freddie Thomas.* Rochester, NY: Brown Publishing, 2015.

Dupree, Adolph, "Rooms full of Promises." *about…time*, February, 1980.

Dupree, Adolph, "Rochester Roots/Routines, Part III." *about…time* August, 1984, 24.

Hill, Laura Warren. *Strike The Hammer; The Black Freedom Struggle in Rochester, New York, 1940 – 1970.* Ithaca, NY: Cornell University Press, 2021.

University of Alabama at Birmingham, "History of Minorities in Medicine," https://www.uab. edu/medicine/diversity/initiatives/minorities/history, June 1, 2022.

Shaw, Hank, "3 Families of the Year; Monroe County Couples Chosen For Succeeding Through Strength," *Democrat and Chronicle* (Rochester, NY), November 16, 1984.

Shaw, Leah, "Rochester Genesee Valley Club Recruiting," *Democrat and Chronicle* (Rochester, NY), January 1, 2016.

Wilson, Louise, "At The Drop Of A Hat," *The Times-Union* (Rochester, NY), October 22, 1968.

Chapter 2: The Freddie Thomas Foundation

Author Unknown, "Triangle Community Center," *Communicade* (Rochester, NY), January 17, 1976.

Author Unknown, "Up, Up, and Away at the Triangle Center (Get the Point?)," *Rochester Patriot* (Rochester, NY), December 16 – January 13, 1982.

Snead, "Triangle Community Center: Minority-Owned Recreational and Cultural Mecca," *About…Time*, August 1978.

Thompson, Shirley, "Freddie Thomas Foundation Celebrates 20th Year," *The Frederick Douglass Voice* (Rochester, NY), November 9, 1994.

Chapter 3: The Triangle Community Center

Author Unknown, "Triangle Center: Unique Role in City," Publication and date unknown.

Author Unknown, "Triangle Community Center," *Communicade* (Rochester, NY), January 17, 1976.

Author Unknown, "Up, Up, and Away at the Triangle Center (Get the Point?)," *Rochester Patriot* (Rochester, NY), December 16 – January 13, 1982.

Dupree, Adolph, "Rooms Full of Promises," *about…time*, February 1980.

Helfer, Andrew, "The Talking Heads Come to Rochester," *Campus Times* (Rochester, NY), November 7, 1978.

Mark , Larry, "Holiday Meals, A Memorial to UR Researcher," *Times-Union* (Rochester, NY), November 26, 1982.

Murphy, Dede, "New Quarters Planned for Displaced YW Residents," *Democrat and Chronicle* (Rochester, NY), May 30, 1981, sec. 3B.

Snead, "Triangle Community Center: Minority-Owned Recreational and Cultural Mecca," *about…time*, August, 1978.

Zelickson, Jill A, "It's 3,000 Square Feet Plus Bingo, Foundation Offering Hall in New Headquarters," *Democrat and Chronicle* (Rochester, NY), March 26, 1994.

Chapter 4: The Miss Jane Pittman Drinking Fountain

Author Unknown, "Drinking Fountain Replica Unveiled," *about…time*, November 1988, 35.

Author Unknown, "The Freddie Thomas Foundation," *Frederick Douglass Voice* (Rochester, NY), August 2 – 14, 1989.

Engle, Dresden D., "Pittman Fountain to Stand For Equality, Freedom," *The Brighton-Pittsford Post* (Rochester, NY), Date unknown.

Chapter 5: The Triangle Square Center

Zelickson, Jill A, "It's 3,000 Square Feet Plus Bingo; Foundation Offering Hall in New Headquarters," *Democrat and Chronicle* (Rochester, NY), March 26, 1994.

Chapter 6: The Dr. Freddie Thomas Learning Center

Benjamin, Cynthia, "Mentoring Can Inspire Families," *Democrat and Chronicle* (Rochester, NY), November 18, 2007.

Buyer, Dan, "City School Board Honors 'Teacher's Teacher' Thomas," *Rochester Free Press* (Rochester, NY), Date unknown.

Ireland, Corydon, "Scio Street School Honors Its Namesake," Publication and date unknown.

Morrell, Alan, "Garden of Flowers Salutes Fallen Cop," *Democrat and Chronicle* (Rochester, NY), September 11, 2003.